ENHANCING TEACHING AND RESEARCH WITH AI

I've been using tools such as ChatGPT and Copilot in my teaching and research for some time, and I can honestly say this book is one I wish I'd had sooner. *Enhancing Teaching and Research with AI: Techniques in LLM Prompt Engineering* is the practical guide lecturers and researchers have been waiting for.

The authors have done an excellent job of focusing on the everyday realities of academic life. They show you how to craft prompts that deliver results, whether you're generating research questions, designing assessments and exams, summarising papers quickly, or creating teaching materials. The step-by-step advice and real-world examples make it easy to apply them straight away, and the sections on iteratively refining prompts and automating routine tasks are particularly strong.

What I appreciated most is that they don't just celebrate the technology. They give proper attention to academic integrity and the ethical use of AI, which feels balanced and thoughtful in today's context.

This is the sort of book that will save people a lot of time and frustration. I'll be recommending it to my colleagues and research students.

—*Anthony Stevenson*, Associate Professor of Accounting and Finance, Heriot-Watt University, Dubai

If you're curious about how generative AI can truly transform your academic work, this book is an inspiring place to start. It brings prompt engineering to life as a powerful scholarly skill, showing how the right questions and instructions can unlock deeper, more meaningful AI-driven insights. At the same time, it affirms the agency of scholars, reminding us that academics remain in control as critical thinkers, creative designers, and responsible knowledge-makers.

Blending practical guidance with a fresh perspective, the book shows how to harness GenAI to enrich teaching, elevate research, and simplify everyday tasks while maintaining intellectual rigor and originality. Engaging, insightful, and highly relevant, it is a must-read for anyone who wants to use AI not just effectively, but thoughtfully and creatively in today's academic world.

—*Anuragini Shirish*, Université Paris-Saclay, Univ Evry, IMT-BS, LITEM, 91025, Evry-Courcouronnes, France

This book is an invaluable tool for academics as we negotiate how to teach and research as effectively as possible in the age of generative AI. With clearly explained concepts and useful examples, the authors make the integration of LLMs accessible across a wide range of disciplines. This book is a must-read for anyone using large-language models who wants to be better at and more efficient with this type of work.

—*Danielle Sarver Coombs*, Ph.D., Ravensbourne University, London

Sinha, Chandra, and Waghmare have created something which is a need of the hour, a resource that is both thorough and easy to use. Their step-by-step approach to prompt engineering, from writing first prompts to refining them, reflects how effective teaching happens. It's a guide for both novices and experts using AI tools in teaching.

The chapter on automation by itself could help a busy lecturer save several hours each week. The section on ethics is also one of the most straightforward and realistic discussions about academic integrity and AI that I have seen in print.

It is not about AI replacing what we do. Rather, their message is far more powerful and, in fact, liberating; by learning to pose better questions with these tools, we will become stronger researchers and educators. The concept that prompt engineering is critical thinking is something that I will take into my own classes.

The success in academia in the coming decades would not be determined by who knew the most about artificial intelligence, but by who started working with it early enough. This book can give you this advantage.

—*Dr Sandhya Prakash*, Associate Professor – Finance and Data Analysis, S P Jain School of Global Management, Singapore

This timely and highly relevant book offers a much-needed bridge between rapidly evolving AI technologies and their practical application in academia. By focusing on prompt engineering for lecturers and researchers, the authors provide clear, structured, and actionable guidance on how to effectively leverage large language models to enhance teaching, streamline research processes, and improve academic productivity.

What distinguishes this book is its strong academic orientation combined with practical utility. Drawing on real-world examples and structured approaches, it empowers educators and scholars to design meaningful prompts that improve learning experiences, support research development, and foster innovation. The emphasis on ethical considerations and responsible AI use further strengthens its value in today's academic environment.

This book will be highly beneficial for lecturers, researchers, and postgraduate students seeking to integrate AI into their workflows in a rigorous and impactful manner. It is a valuable contribution to the growing field of AI-enabled education and research.

—*Tristan Chong*, PhD, Professor and Area Head of Marketing, S P Jain School of Global Management, Singapore

ENHANCING TEACHING AND RESEARCH WITH AI

Techniques in LLM Prompt Engineering

BY

EKTA SINHA
Regent's University London, UK

SHALINI CHANDRA
S P Jain School of Global Management, Singapore

AND

CHARLES DAVID WAGHMARE
Shell, Bangalore, India

emerald
PUBLISHING

United Kingdom – North America – Japan – India
Malaysia – China

Emerald Publishing Limited
Emerald Publishing, Floor 5, Northspring, 21-23 Wellington Street, Leeds LS1 4DL.

First edition 2026

British Library Cataloguing in Publication Data
A catalogue record for this book is available from the British Library

ISBN: 978-1-83742-180-0 (Print)
ISBN: 978-1-83742-179-4 (Online)
ISBN: 978-1-83742-181-7 (Epub)

Printed and bound by CPI Group (UK) Ltd, Croydon, CR0 4YY

INVESTOR IN PEOPLE

This book is dedicated to the loving memory of my late father, Shri Anil Kumar Sinha, whose values and guidance continue to inspire me … my shining star! (E.S.)

In fond remembrance, I would like to dedicate this book to my loving mother, the late Mrs Padma Srivastava, whose guiding light always stays with me. (S.C.)

I wish to express my heartfelt gratitude to the following individuals who have profoundly impacted my life:

The late Mr Anil Malvankar, former Deputy General Manager at SIEMENS, who graciously offered me my first professional opportunity at SIEMENS. His mentorship and guidance were invaluable, and I remain deeply appreciative of his support until his passing in April 2024.

The late Mr Alwin Fernandis, my cherished friend. Though he is no longer with us, his memory endures in my heart, and his influence continues to inspire me. (C.D.W.)

CONTENTS

ACKNOWLEDGEMENTS

EKTA SINHA

This book has been shaped by a journey of intellectual exploration, reflection, and sustained effort, and I am deeply grateful to those who have supported me along the way.

By the grace of almighty, I would like to take this opportunity to express my deepest gratitude to my family, whose support has been the foundation of this endeavour. To my mother, Smt. Kanchana Sinha, for her unwavering strength and quiet encouragement, which has guided me more than words can express. To my husband, Rakesh, for his patience, belief, and constant support through many phases of this project and beyond. To my lifeline – my son – who has been a source of joy and perspective, reminding me of what truly matters beyond work. And to my siblings, for their encouragement, warmth, and presence in my life ... I couldn't have done without you!

I would also like to acknowledge my colleagues and students who have continually challenged my thinking and enriched my understanding of teaching, research, and the evolving role of artificial intelligence in academia. Their insights, questions, and engagement have been invaluable in shaping the ideas presented in this work.

Special thanks to my friends who never fail to uplift my spirits!!!

Last but not least, I would like to thank my co-authors – Prof. Shalini Chandra and Charles David Waghmare, for their constant belief, support, and invaluable contribution in shaping this humble attempt to help academics engage with large language models in their work.

SHALINI CHANDRA

With extreme gratitude, I would like to acknowledge the support of my family and colleagues, who made conceptualising and authoring this book a memorable experience.

First and foremost, I would like to acknowledge the encouragement and confidence I received from my father, Prof. Suresh Chandra Srivastava. As an academic himself, he was always ready to listen to my challenges and gave me the inner strength to author this book. I gratefully acknowledge the love and support I received from my husband, Vibhu, which boosted my self-confidence and impressed upon me the value of willpower. I want to thank my loving kids, Vashita and Vansh, for their unconditional love and support. Finally, my special thanks go to my mentor and co-author on several research papers, Dr Shirish C. Srivastava, who provided invaluable guidance and support and inspired me to author this book by highlighting the need for a book for teachers and researchers on this very critical topic in the current generative artificial intelligence era.

CHARLES DAVID WAGHMARE

"Blessed are those who find wisdom, those who gain understanding." – Proverbs 3:13

To begin, I want to express my gratitude to Lord Jesus Christ for giving me another chance to author this book. I attribute all my achievements to Him and use this moment to offer praise and thanks for everything. He has done in my life. God bless.

This book will always hold a special place in my heart, as I penned this book during the time my dear father, the late Mr David Genuji Waghmare, passed away. I dedicate this work to both my beloved father and my beloved late mother, Mrs Kamala David Waghmare, who departed for their heavenly abode within three years of each other.

I thank my parents for their lasting impact on my life and career and for their continued support. I also dedicate this book to my wife, Mrs Priya Waghmare, for her unwavering love and encouragement.

1

INTRODUCTION OF GEN AI AND PROMPT ENGINEERING FOR LECTURERS AND RESEARCHERS

ABSTRACT

Prompt engineering is a vital technique in artificial intelligence (AI), especially when interacting with AI models. It involves designing precise, context-rich prompts to effectively guide AI responses. The quality of AI outputs – whether in relevance, clarity, or accuracy – depends heavily on how well prompts are crafted. Understanding an AI model's capabilities and limitations is crucial for creating effective prompts, as different models excel in different areas, such as creativity or information retrieval. Clear and specific prompts yield better results. For instance, asking 'Explain the significance of black holes in astrophysics' is more effective than a vague 'Tell me about space'. Providing context – such as background information or previous conversation details – enhances the AI's comprehension. Prompt engineering is often iterative; refining prompts based on initial responses yields better outcomes. Experimentation is key. Trying different prompt styles helps users understand how AI interprets inputs and allows for better customisation. In academic settings, prompt engineering plays a transformative role. It enables AI to assist in learning, teaching, and research by making education more personalised and innovative. AI can summarise academic articles, generate research questions, and synthesise complex information, saving time and enhancing understanding. For example, it can distil key findings from journals or generate questions on topics such as renewable energy. In writing,

AI supports thesis development, logical structuring, language refinement, and improving clarity and adherence to academic standards. Overall, integrating AI into academic workflows boosts productivity, fosters creativity, and deepens insight, making it a powerful partner in education and research.

Keywords: Artificial intelligence; machine learning; deep learning; Gen AI systems; sentiment analysis; natural language processing; large language models; embeddings; fine tuning

Chapter Goal: Understanding AI and prompt engineering fundamentals

1. INTRODUCTION

In recent years, advances in AI have had a profound impact on academia and research. Thus, as educators and researchers, understanding the nuances of this AI technology is pivotal not only for leveraging its potential but also for guiding students and peers in utilising these tools. This chapter introduces the fundamental concepts of Generative AI (Gen AI) and prompt engineering, setting the stage for their practical application in academic contexts.

2. PRECURSOR TO GEN AI AND PROMPT ENGINEERING

Generative AI, often referred to as Gen AI, represents a quick surge in the capabilities of AI. Unlike traditional AI systems designed for specific tasks, such as Google Maps predicting travel time, social media advertisements, and Tesla's self-driving cars, Gen AI goes one step further by offering generative capabilities. Gen AI, being a combination of generative and AI, can create new content, including text, images, and even music. For example, we can use ChatGPT to generate text, such as an email for us, rather than pulling one from a file. Similarly, we can use DALL-E, another Gen AI model, to generate an image of my favourite pet or use GitHub Copilot, an extension of GitHub, to write a code snippet for me. All these examples involve 'generating' new content rather than retrieving it from a file or document. Thus, contrary to the academic uses of traditional AI systems for categorising data and detecting sentiment in a sentence for analysis and prediction, Gen AI is increasingly used by educators and researchers to generate content such as images, text, audio, source code, and video.

As a precursor to learning Gen AI and prompt engineering, we need to understand:

- What is AI or artificial intelligence?
- How does machine learning (ML) work?
- Differentiate between AI, ML, and deep learning (DL).

2.1. Artificial Intelligence

Humans are the most intelligent species ever to have existed on Earth, excelling in all areas, including science, the arts, and sports. This is real 'human' intelligence. When we intend to replicate human intelligence in a machine, meaning we are trying to make a machine as smart and intelligent as a human being, that is called AI. In the 1950s and 1960s, AI was primarily rule-based, relying on explicit programming to perform tasks. For example, early chess programs used predefined rules to make a move.

Thus, AI is a broad field of computer science focused on creating intelligent systems capable of performing tasks that typically require human intelligence. In other words, AI is the simulation of human intelligence processes by machines, including learning, reasoning, and self-correction (Russell & Norvig, 2010). For example, creating AI systems that can diagnose diseases from X-rays, predict property prices, or even detect credit card fraud. Although these tasks require typical human intelligence, they can be performed by incorporating human-like intelligence in machines, known as AI.

2.2. Machine Learning

The next big question is: 'How can machines become as intelligent as human beings?' Historically, AI began with rule-based systems that mimicked human decision-making processes (Russell & Norvig, 2010). Over time, by the 1980s and 1990s, the focus shifted to ML, where systems learned patterns from data rather than relying on rule-based programming (Mitchell, 1997). A classic example is the spam filter, which learns to identify spam emails by extracting features from a large dataset.

ML is a subset of AI that focuses on developing algorithms and models that enable computers to learn and make predictions or decisions without explicit programming from humans. The key objective of ML is to train machines to make predictions or decisions by learning on their own, without requiring explicit human programming. Thus, as the name suggests, ML involves making machines learn. It involves using algorithms to parse data, learn from it, and make informed decisions based on that learning. In other words, ML trains the machine to learn about things and then enables it to make predictions or perform other tasks without human involvement.

The basic concept of ML is like how humans learn. For example, a child learns to differentiate an apple from other fruits by repeatedly learning that the round red fruit is an apple and different from a banana or an orange. Gradually, they can confidently identify an apple from other fruits in a fruit basket. Another example is to use ML to assist radiologists in diagnosing diseases by analysing medical images, such as X-rays or MRIs, to identify conditions like pneumonia or tumours. ML requires the following:

Lots of training data to equip machines with the same level of intelligence as humans. Though humans can easily recognise an object, machines need to be trained on millions of images of that object, with varying colours, variants, and sizes, to achieve a similar level of accuracy.

Significant computational power to process massive amounts of data, computations, and optimisations. Earlier ML models were limited by the available computational power. However, computational power has increased significantly, thanks to the low cost and widespread availability of graphics processing units for training complex AI models, which can process massive datasets in parallel.

Solid algorithms to process all the information, learn from training data, identify patterns, attributes, clusters, and predict results without human intervention.

2.3. Deep Learning

The 2010s saw the rise of DL as the next iteration of ML, enabling AI to perform complex tasks such as image and speech recognition. DL is a subset of ML, but it is grounded in the principles of human neural systems. DL uses neural networks with many layers (hence 'deep') to analyse various factors of data (LeCun et al., 2015). The human body transmits information through a network of neurons. These neurons form multiple layers, each connected to the others, and they process information. Thus, if a human uses their eyes to see an object, say, a dog, their neurons transmit information to one another, and eventually it reaches their brain, helping them analyse the object and recognise it as a dog. They transmit information through multiple stages and

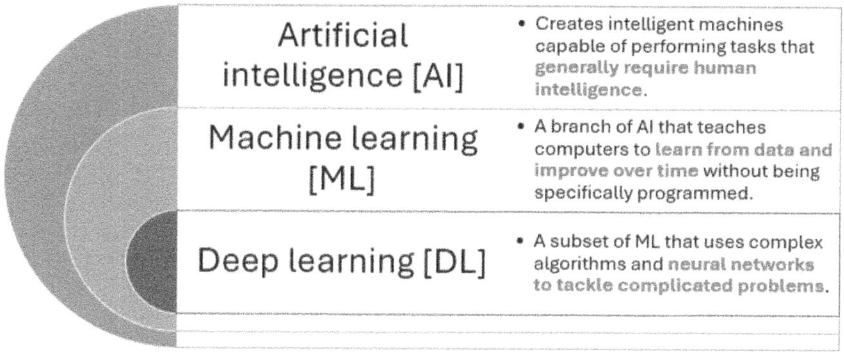

Fig. 1. Relation Between AI, ML, and DL.

layers, each processing, enhancing, and sending it to the next, which eventually makes humans so intelligent. DL replicates this concept of human neurons in ML by creating neural networks.

Thus, DL is a subset of ML that focuses on teaching machines to learn and make decisions by processing data through neural networks inspired by the human brain. It uses multiple-layer neural networks for analysis. Because the training data passes through several layers, each layer analyses it, performs computations on it, learns from it, and predicts; as a result, its accuracy on complex tasks such as text generation improves significantly. Consequently, it produces much more accurate results for complex problems, thereby improving the overall output. Fig. 1 presents the relation between AI, ML, and DL.

2.4. Generative AI

Gen AI emerged as a natural progression, leveraging DL techniques to generate content indistinguishable from that created by humans (Banh & Strobel, 2023). Generative tools such as OpenAI's GPT series use DL neural networks to learn from training data and generate human-like text. Thus, Gen AI is a subset of DL (see Fig. 2).

2.4.1. Key Characteristics of Gen AI Systems

Gen AI trains on *large volumes of data* to achieve accurate results. Gen AI follows the Garbage In, Garbage Out principle of ML models. If the machine trains on bad (garbage) data, then the results are bad (bad). On the other hand, feeding the machines with good data with variations and large volumes gives accurate (good) results. Next, Gen AI requires significant computational

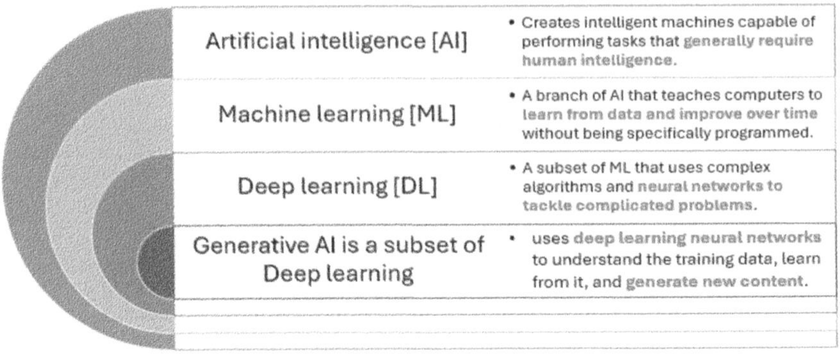

Fig. 2. Gen AI as a Subset of DL.

power because it processes large volumes of data, leverages complex neural networks, and delivers results quickly. Finally, Gen AI has made a clear shift towards ***conversational interaction*** with contextual understanding. Users expect Gen AI to understand context and provide direct answers to their questions.

2.4.2. Difference Between Conventional AI and Gen AI Systems

The key difference between Gen AI and conventional AI systems is their ability to generate new content. In conventional AI systems, we provide training data; the model learns from it and then develops the ability to make predictions, classify data, perform language processing (e.g., translation), or perform computer vision (e.g., image identification). Gen AI, on the other hand, can generate new content (e.g., text, video, and images) based on training data and neural networks.

2.4.3. Examples of Gen AI Applications

Some examples of Gen AI applications across various domains include the following:

Text generation using ChatGPT – initially built on the GPT-3.5 series (Generative Pre-trained Transformer 3.5), a powerful, large-scale language model developed by OpenAI and released in 2020. It can generate human-like text, such as writing essays, answering questions, and even creating poetry based on prompts (Brown et al., 2020). ChatGPT is a language model built on top of OpenAI's GPT-3.5, an improved, fine-tuned version of GPT-3. It is designed for natural language understanding and generation, specifically in a conversational context. Thus, ChatGPT is an AI system that is designed for natural language understanding and generation. The newer versions of ChatGPT built on GPT-4 can generate images. It excels at natural language and is good at understanding and replying in human language; it understands the patterns, structure, and context of the question posed and generates accurate answers. Its key strength lies in handling conversational context by remembering the background of a conversation.

Image generation, using DALL-E, is a model developed by OpenAI that can generate images from textual descriptions and create unique and imaginative visuals, such as fantasy environments, whimsical art pieces, and unconventional characters and creatures (Ramesh et al., 2021).

Music composition using Jukedeck or OpenAI's MuseNet is an AI tool capable of composing original music tracks based on user preferences and generating music in various styles and genres, blending instruments and compositions (Payne, 2019).

Voice synthesis using Google's WaveNet is a deep generative model developed by DeepMind that can produce human-like speech and help improve the naturalness of voice assistants like Google Assistant (Oord et al., 2016).

Art creation using DeepArt and Google's DeepDream – which use neural networks to apply artistic styles to images, transform photos into artworks that resonate with famous painters, and enhance patterns in images to create dream-like visuals (Gatys et al., 2016).

Fashion designing using Generative Adversarial Networks to design new clothing patterns and styles and help fashion designers explore innovative styles (Yan et al., 2022).

Video game content generation using AI Dungeon – an AI-powered interactive text-based adventure game that enables players to interact using natural language and create and explore innovative storylines (Walton, 2020).

Though Gen AI is disrupting all industries, this book focuses specifically on its effectiveness for learning, teaching, and research in the education sector.

2.5. Gen AI Systems Used by Lecturers and Researchers to Improve Experience

Gen AI has the potential to revolutionise the way lecturers and researchers approach writing tasks. Educators and researchers can integrate AI tools into various stages of the writing process to enhance creativity, improve efficiency, and maintain high standards of academic integrity. Thus, Gen AI is transforming the education milieu by equipping lecturers and researchers with innovative tools that enhance their productivity and creativity to unprecedented levels. Educators are utilising Gen AI models for several applications, such as:

- Brainstorming and generating research ideas on new topics using Gen AI tools such as ChatGPT, where the researcher inputs a general topic, and the AI generates suggestions for research ideas on that topic (Eymann et al., 2025).
- Generating lecture notes, quizzes, and lesson plans using Gen AI models like OpenAI's GPT-3. Thus, lecturers can focus more on teaching interactively and automate content preparation (Brown et al., 2020).
- Editing and refining the draft paper for clarity and readability using AI tools such as Grammarly (AlAfnan, 2025).
- Drafting sections of research papers, summarising literature, and extracting key points and references using Gen AI tools such as Scholarcy, which saves researchers significant time (Cohan et al., 2018).
- Analysing large datasets and generating visualisations using Gen AI tools such as IBM's Watson Studio to draw new insights and present data effectively (Norouzi et al., 2025).
- Creating inclusive learning environments by using Gen AI models like Google's Bidirectional Encoder Representations from Transformers (BERT) to translate educational materials into multiple languages and increase their accessibility to non-native speakers (Devlin et al., 2019).
- Creating personalised language-learning experiences using Gen AI-driven platforms such as Duolingo to provide a customised learning experience for learners (Von Ahn, 2013).
- Serving as virtual teaching assistants to answer student queries and provide feedback by integrating AI-powered chatbots such as IBM Watson Assistant into educational platforms for enhanced student engagement (Adamopoulou & Moussiades, 2020).

- Detecting plagiarism in student submissions using Gen AI tools like Turnitin and using AI responsibly for their research to maintain academic integrity (Canyakan, 2025).

3. BASICS OF GEN AI

Gen AI represents a transformative approach in AI, focusing on generating new content rather than merely analysing existing data. This section explores the foundational elements of Gen AI, including natural language processing (NLP), large language models (LLMs), embeddings, fine-tuning, and a specific focus on GPT (Generative Pre-trained Transformer), each playing a pivotal role in Gen AI applications. They hold immense potential to transform academic practices. A clear understanding of these technologies can help lecturers and researchers enhance their own work and prepare their students for an AI-driven world.

3.1. Natural Language Processing

NLP is a subfield of AI that focuses on human-computer interaction through natural language. NLP enables machines to understand, interpret, and generate human language in a meaningful and useful manner. NLP has been widely used in AI-driven educational applications, as elaborated below.

3.1.1. Sentiment Analysis

Sentiment analysis is the process of determining the sentiment in a text section, such as customer reviews or social media posts. Traditionally, sentiment analysis uses *lexicon-based approaches* that rely on predefined lists of words associated with positive or negative sentiment (Giatsoglou et al., 2017). However, this approach is insufficient to capture context-specific meanings. With the advent of ML and DL, machines are increasingly applying these approaches to classify text by sentiment. Such models can capture more complex patterns and understand context and dependencies in text, resulting in more accurate sentiment predictions (Minaee et al., 2021). It has several applications for lecturers and researchers.

First, one key application of sentiment analysis for teaching purposes is analysing student feedback collected by universities and colleges on courses, instructors, and the overall student experience. This facilitates data-driven decisions to enhance course offerings and teaching methods (Jim et al., 2024).

Second, it can be useful for researchers by applying it to a corpus of academic publications to gauge the sentiment of scholarly discourse (Mäntylä et al., 2018).

Third, sentiment analysis is often used by researchers to analyse tweets and comments to assess public sentiment towards their research findings and to understand how their work is perceived (Boon-Itt & Skunkan, 2020).

Finally, sentiment analysis is often used by lecturers to evaluate user feedback on educational technologies used as teaching aids, gauge user satisfaction, and identify areas for improvement (Mondal et al., 2024).

3.1.2. Large Language Models

LLMs are advanced NLP models trained on large amounts of text data and designed to understand and generate human-like text. These AI models are built on DL architectures, specifically transformers, that facilitate the process and generate text with excellent accuracy and rationality. Roughly, an LLM can be explained as a predictive text feature that predicts the next word or sentence, helping users complete their responses in email and messaging services. Thus, LLMs can understand, process, and generate text by accurately determining words, grammar, sentences, and context. Though Gen AI broadly refers to generating text, images, audio, video, code snippets, and others, LLMs deal only with generating text.

3.1.2.1. How Does an LLM Work? LLMs are DL models that leverage massive text datasets and advanced neural networks to process and generate human language. They have been developed to address the need for models that can understand context, capture semantic subtleties, and perform a variety of language tasks with minimal human intervention. LLMs are characterised by their large number of parameters (which can reach the billions), enabling them to capture complex language patterns.

The foundational architecture for LLMs is a specific type of neural network, the transformer, which enables them to process sequences of text efficiently and model long-range dependencies (Vaswani et al., 2017). Transformers are architectures trained on large amounts of data, enabling them to understand language, meaning, and context in text easily (Wolf et al., 2020). For example, ChatGPT is an LLM trained on Wikipedia, websites, blogs, and manuals, thus developing excellent capabilities to understand text and deliver outputs (Ray, 2023). Also note that ChatGPT repeatedly generates one word at a time, producing the long sentences and paragraphs we see (see Fig. 3).

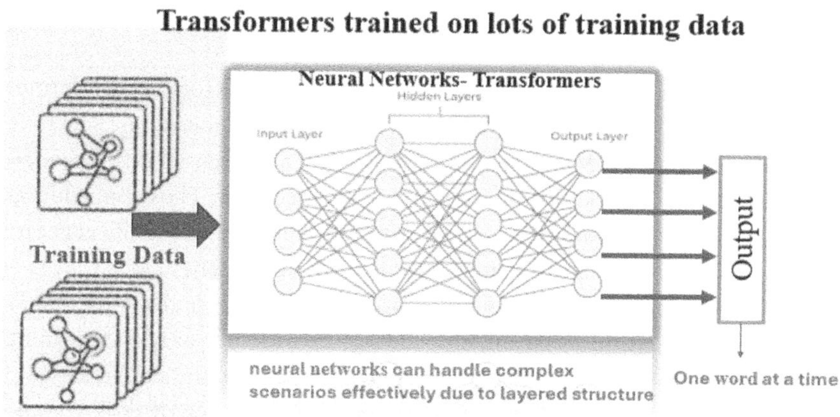

Fig. 3. The Concept Behind LLMs.

In summary, LLMs are pre-trained on large corpora to understand a wide range of words, grammar, sentences, and text semantics. This helps LLMs train more effectively and improve their output accuracy. Because LLMs use massive neural networks known as transformers and are trained on billions of parameters, their understanding and generation capabilities are enhanced.

3.1.2.2. Examples of LLM Applications LLMs have set new benchmarks in language understanding and generation. Some prominent examples are GPT and BERT (Brown et al., 2020).

GPT-3 by OpenAI is a state-of-the-art LLM with several billion parameters, capable of generating human-like text across multiple language tasks, such as content creation, code generation, and interactive episodes, with minimal input (Brown et al., 2020).

BERT by Google is another prominent LLM designed using a bidirectional training approach to understand the context of words in a sentence, enhance its language understanding capabilities, and improve tasks such as sentiment analysis and translation (Devlin et al., 2019)

LLMs like OpenAI's ChatGPT and Meta AI's LLaMA are used across industries, including marketing, sales, and advertising, to generate text content (Chkirbene et al., 2024). Chatbots, or virtual assistants, are also LLMs used for user interactions and support, answering questions based on the company's documentation (Chandra et al., 2022). Further, LLMs are being used for language translation, facilitating conversational chat for better results (Duan et al., 2024). Finally, LLMs are being used to summarise lengthy text content, answer questions, and provide information (Xie et al., 2025).

3.2. Embeddings

In NLP, embeddings are numerical representations (vectors in a continuous vector space) of words or phrases that depict their meanings, semantic nuances, and contexts (Mikolov et al., 2013). They are essential for AI models to understand and work with human language effectively. Thus, embeddings help convert text into numbers so that LLMs can understand it, generate more text around it, or answer questions about it accurately.

Unlike traditional encoding, which represents words as numbers or sparse vectors with limited information, embeddings provide not only the meaning of a word or sentence but also its usage context, capturing the similarities and differences between words based on their usage in language (Mikolov et al., 2013). For example, read the two sentences below:

This teacher is 'super'.

This teacher is always late to class, 'super'.

The word 'super' has been used in two different contexts, and embeddings should be able to convey not only the meaning of the word or sentence but also the context of use. Thus, embedding employs a two-step process: the first step is to chunk words into tokens, and the second is to train LLMs to generate embeddings that capture meaning, context, and relationships (Fig. 4).

Thus, embeddings are driving advancements in language understanding and processing by enabling machines to capture the semantic and contextual meanings of language. Embeddings enable more accurate search results and recommendations by understanding the semantic meaning of queries and information and by capturing user preferences and subject characteristics. Thus, by representing text as numbers or vectors, embeddings allow many applications ranging from semantic search to sentiment analysis (Mikolov et al., 2013).

3.2.1. Types of Embeddings

Word2Vec, developed by Google, uses neural networks to learn associations among words from large amounts of data, producing word vectors that capture semantic similarities (Mikolov et al., 2013).

GloVe (Global Vectors for Word Representation), developed at Stanford, generates word embeddings using an unsupervised learning algorithm that aggregates global word–word co-occurrence statistics from a large corpus (Pennington et al., 2014).

BERT generates dynamic embeddings that interpret the context of a word within a sentence (Devlin et al., 2019).

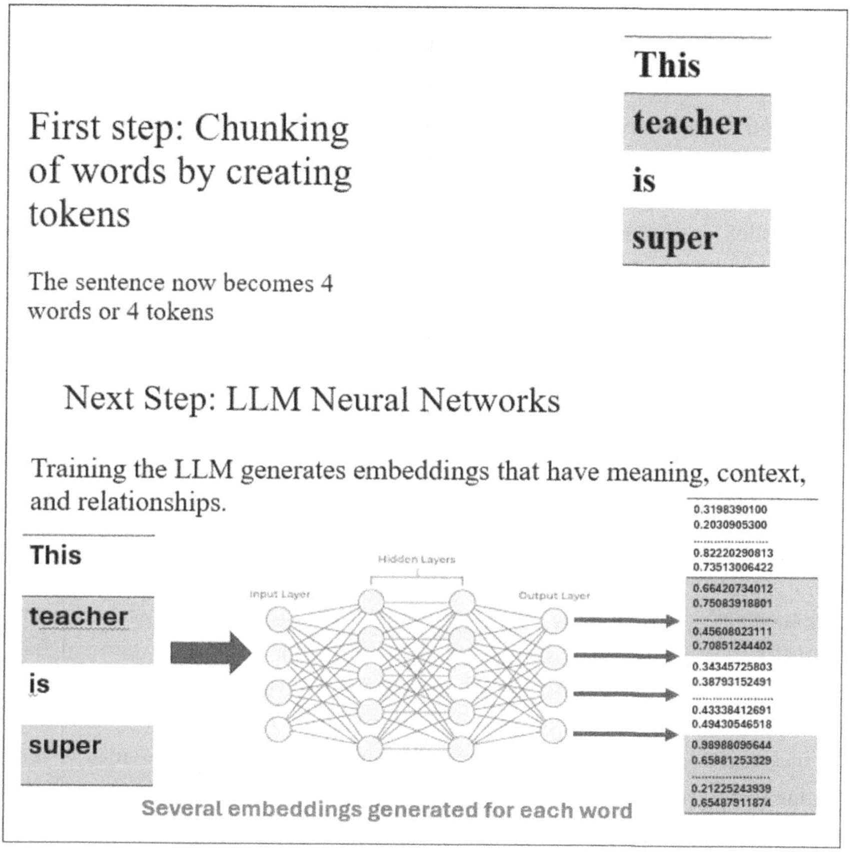

Fig. 4. Two-step Process in Embeddings.

3.3. Fine-tuning

LLMs like ChatGPT, LLaMA, Gemini, and Claude are pre-trained on large datasets, enabling them to perform effectively and provide accurate answers to a wide range of questions. However, this is generic training.

If we need to generate information about a specific task or dataset within an organisation, we will have to train the model on that dataset. This is called fine-tuning. Thus, fine-tuning is the process of customising pre-trained models for specific tasks. Though LLMs are pre-trained, they can be fine-tuned on a more specific, task-oriented dataset. Thus, if we want to use an LLM for text completion or summarisation, we need to fine-tune it by exposing it to data from these tasks. For example, if we intend to get accurate, contextually relevant responses from our LLM to questions about our university curriculum, we need to train it on relevant datasets to generate content that meets students' needs. Thus, fine-tuning is the process of adapting a pre-trained AI model to accomplish a specific task or context, such as fine-tuning an LLM on medical data or academic data (Howard & Ruder, 2018). Fine-tuning an LLM on a domain-specific dataset improves its accuracy (see Fig. 5).

Fine-tuning helps LLMs specialise in specific tasks by learning task-specific patterns while reducing the computational resources and time required to train models from scratch (Howard & Ruder, 2018); for example, fine-tuning a pre-trained LLM on a movie review dataset to accurately predict viewers' sentiments (Howard & Ruder, 2018). Similarly, fine-tuning an LLM on a dataset of annotated text can help with text classification, such as classifying entities (e.g., names, dates, and locations) (Alizadeh et al., 2025). There are three specific ways to fine-tune an LLM.

3.3.1. Self-supervised Fine-tuning

Self-supervised learning is a type of unsupervised learning in which an LLM learns to predict parts of the input from other parts of the input. Thus, in self-supervised fine-tuning, we provide the foundation LLM with massive amounts of domain-specific training data, enabling it to learn general language representations from the inherent structure of the data and generate missing content (Devlin et al., 2019). For example, if we say 'I ___ tea' then the model knows that the missing word is 'drink' (see Fig. 6). The idea is very similar to pre-training an LLM; however, the key difference is that the model is fine-tuned on a domain-specific dataset.

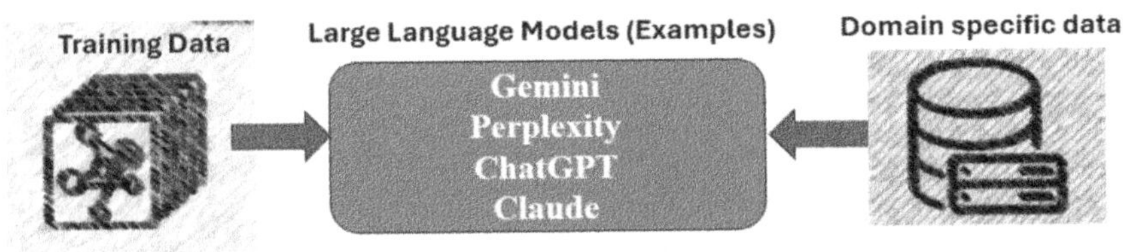

Fig. 5. Fine-tuning.

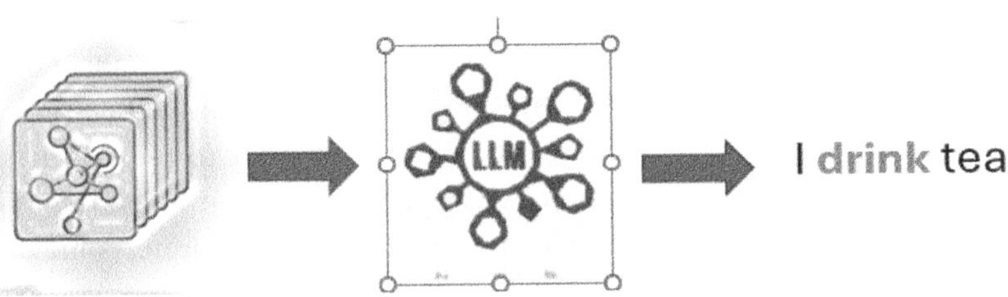

Fig. 6. Example of Self-supervised Fine-tuning.

A common example of self-supervised learning is masked language modelling, used in models like BERT. It involves masked language modelling and next-sentence prediction to help models understand syntax, semantics, and context, generate labels without manually labelled data, and predict missing data (Devlin et al., 2019; Jeong, 2024; Liu et al., 2019). During pre-training, BERT learns to predict masked words in a sentence based on their context, thereby extracting semantic and syntactic information (Devlin et al., 2019). Thus, if we want to train the model on an educational dataset so that students can generate content tailored to their specific needs and use it to deepen their knowledge of specific subjects, we need to provide the curriculum structure, learning objectives, and all documents related to students and subjects.

3.3.2. Supervised Fine-tuning

Supervised fine-tuning involves providing detailed, labelled training data with input and output so the model can learn from it. This approach involves training the model on a labelled dataset, where each input is paired with a corresponding output label. It is widely used for tasks where labelled data is readily available, such as classification and regression (Goodfellow et al., 2016). For example, we may have a labelled dataset with an input query such as 'Which is the smallest planet in our solar system?' and an output of 'Mercury' (see Fig. 7). Thus, in supervised fine-tuning, we provide the pre-trained model with labelled datasets specific to the target task, which it learns from and improves upon.

For example, fine-tuning BERT on the IMDb movie reviews dataset to predict the sentiment of each review involves adjusting its parameters to classify text as positive, negative, or neutral using labelled examples (Sun et al., 2019).

3.3.3. Reinforcement Learning Fine-tuning

Reinforcement learning is basically a feedback-based learning method. Reinforcement learning fine-tuning involves training a model to predict by interacting with an environment and receiving feedback in the form of rewards or

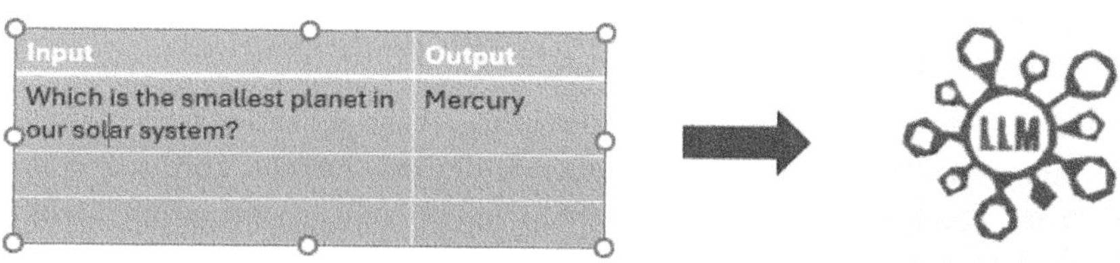

Fig. 7. Example of Supervised Fine-tuning with Labelled Training Data.

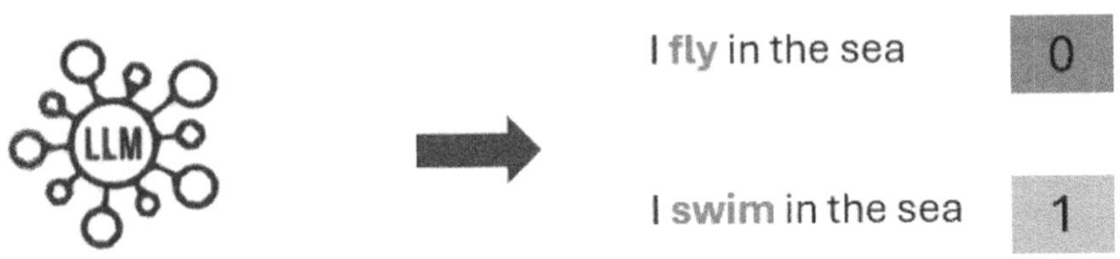

Fig. 8. Example of Reinforcement Learning Fine-tuning.

penalties. Thus, the model generates some output based on its training. It is a useful fine-tuning method for tasks in which the model must learn a sequence of actions to achieve a goal (Sutton & Barto, 1998).

The concept of reinforcement involves assigning a high score to a good response and a low score to a bad one. For example, if a professor instructs a student to complete an assignment and the student diligently follows the instruction, the student earns a high score. On the other hand, if the student fails to follow the instructions, the professor will give a low score. Over time, the student realises how to get rewarded and begins to follow that action. Similarly, the model generates output based on its training, and if the output is poor, we assign a low score; if it's good, we assign a high score (see Fig. 8). Over time, the model learns to predict more accurately based on high/low scores.

Thus, in reinforcement learning fine-tuning, the model learns over time the basis for high and low scores and accordingly fine-tunes its predictions to improve accuracy. Summarising, fine-tuning is not about creating a model from scratch or replacing existing knowledge. Rather, it involves starting with a foundation model pre-trained on large datasets and fine-tuning it with a domain-specific dataset to achieve more accurate results. Finally, fine-tuning is an iterative process due to the variability of tasks, data, and use cases. Multiple cycles of fine-tuning may be required before getting satisfactory results. For example, OpenAI's ChatGPT applies reinforcement learning and fine-tunes with human feedback to optimise its responses and provide helpful, engaging responses preferred by humans (Stiennon et al., 2020).

4. PROMPT ENGINEERING

Prompt engineering, a relatively new discipline, is the art and science of crafting inputs that guide AI models to generate desired outputs. This skill is the core component of Gen AI and essential for maximising its utility. Unlike traditional programming, where specific instructions are provided, prompt engineering relies on natural-language prompts to shape AI model behaviour.

Prompt engineering is particularly relevant for LLMs like GPT-3, which are designed to understand and generate human-like text based on the prompts they receive (Brown et al., 2020). It is significant because it directly influences the quality and relevance of AI-generated content.

As AI models are gaining momentum across a diverse range of applications spanning content creation to customer service, the ability to engineer effective prompts is valuable (Reynolds & McDonell, 2021). Hence, before we understand how to engineer an effective prompt, let us first understand what a prompt is.

4.1. What Is a Prompt?

Asking a question or giving an instruction and input to get the desired response is a prompt (Arora et al., 2022). For example, when we talk to Alexa and ask a question – 'What is the recipe for chocolate cookies?' or ask Google, 'What is the nutritional value of a banana?' or ask Siri, 'Is it going to be a sunny day tomorrow?' – these are prompts. Thus, a prompt is a specific question, command, or input we provide to an AI system to request an explicit response, a specific piece of information, or a discrete action.

The key purpose of prompts is to generate accurate, relevant, and contextually appropriate responses from AI models. Prompts help ensure that the AI model understands and responds correctly to user inputs. They are used in various applications, including chatbots, automated customer service, content creation, and more. Some examples of prompts include asking Gen AI to summarise a research article and how it can be applied to a specific industry, or for creative writing, such as writing a short poem for an event, or generating an image using Dall-E, such as an inspirational character for the fitness industry, or even generating Python code for some mathematical computation using GitHub Copilot.

4.2. Why Do We Need Prompt Engineering?

Prompt engineering involves creating and refining inputs (prompts) to guide the output of NLP models like GPT-4o. Prompt engineering helps contextualise our queries. For example, if I ask my friend a generic question without any context, such as:

What is the weather in Manila?

Then I will get a generic response from my friend.

However, if I change it to a more specific and contextualised question, such as:

> *I am going on a business trip to Manila next Monday. What will be the weather then?*

Your friend may tell you that it has been raining for the past few days and there is a tsunami warning. The general tendency for us humans is to give more information, such as the traffic to the city might be delayed, so you may want to be prepared with extra time to reach your conference venue on time.

Thus, if we ask clear, specific, and accurate questions in our prompt, we provide the correct context and tend to get better responses. Thus, prompt engineering is the process of crafting well-defined, structured queries to interact with AI systems and obtain accurate, relevant responses. It is important as it directly impacts the quality and relevance of AI-generated content. Further, it ensures that the AI model understands and responds correctly to user inputs. Engineering effective prompts is the key in academic contexts where precision and relevance are paramount. Thoughtfully crafted prompts yield strong, compelling, and coherent responses, whereas ill-crafted prompts result in unrelated, illogical, or irrelevant outputs. Because prompt engineering generates accurate, relevant, and contextually appropriate responses from AI models, it is used across applications such as chatbots, automated customer service, content creation, and more.

4.3. Step-by-Step Process for Creating Prompts

- *Define the goal* – to understand what you want the Gen AI to achieve.
- *Create initial prompts* – starting with a simple prompt.
- *Test and refine the output* to evaluate and adjust.
- *Iterate* and continuously refine the prompt based on feedback.

4.4. Few Challenges with Prompt Engineering

- *Results may be inconsistent*, and a small change in your prompt can alter them.
- *You cannot fit too many things into a prompt.* Too many instructions and pieces of information in a prompt can confuse and lead to inaccurate results.
- *To achieve accurate results* for your specific corpus, fine-tuning is essential.

4.5. Common Pitfalls in Prompt Engineering and How to Avoid Them

Prompts that are too broad or unclear result in vagueness. The *prompts should be clear* and straightforward. Next, overly complex prompts that confuse the AI model. *Simplify complex prompts* by breaking them down into simpler parts. Finally, a biased prompt may lead the AI model to generate biased responses. You should *be aware of potential biases* and the neutrality test.

4.6. Best Practices for Prompt Engineering

Prompt engineering is an art that requires only simple English, not coding. The AI model remembers the prompt and provides a customised output (Marvin et al., 2023). The best practices for effective prompt design include the following.

4.6.1. Initial Prompts Should Balance Simplicity and Complexity

Define the goal to convey the desired response and avoid ambiguities. Although simple prompts yield wide, generic answers, complex prompts may confuse the LLM, leading to irrelevant responses. When designing initial prompts, maintain a fair balance between overly simple and overly complex prompts. Clearly convey the desired response to avoid any ambiguities. LLMs such as ChatGPT can often give lengthy responses, and the information can become vague. Be very clear in defining the goal to avoid ambiguity.

Defining the goal by providing context or background information. Provide sufficient context to guide the AI model in generating relevant responses. Thus, remember to provide context or background information in your prompts to get answers relevant to that exact context. Be specific about what you want the AI model to do to get accurate results. Use examples to illustrate the desired type of response.

4.6.2. Iterative Testing and Refinement to Achieve Effective Prompt Design

Prompt engineering does not have one single rule that fits all. It is an art to be creative and clear and not just science. It is not easy to get the right prompt in the first step itself, so keep testing, refining, and iterating the responses till you get the best response for your use case. The key steps to achieve interactive testing and refinement include:

- Test the prompts with different inputs to ensure consistency.
- Incorporate feedback from multiple sources to improve prompt quality.
- Keep a record of prompts and their effectiveness for future reference.
- Finally, collaborate with others to brainstorm and refine prompts.

4.7. Applications of Prompt Engineering for Teaching and Research

Prompt engineering is revolutionising practically all industries. It is being used in the services sector, such as banking and e-commerce, to provide customer support by automating responses to common customer queries (Arugula, 2025). Furthermore, it is used in the marketing, media, and communications industries to generate articles, marketing materials, and social media posts (Jasmine, 2024). Further, it is widely used in teaching and research to develop interactive learning materials, summarise large datasets, analyse data, and generate reports (Serra & Oliveira, 2025; Qian, 2025). We discuss the applications for prompt engineering, specifically for lecturers and researchers.

4.7.1. Supplement Teaching Material

Prompt engineering is relevant for lecturers to develop interactive learning materials and enhance educational content. Educators and lecturers can use prompt engineering to generate lecture notes, quizzes, and study guides. By crafting prompts tailored to a specific curriculum, AI models can generate educational materials that align with their learning objectives (Eager & Brunton, 2023). Example: 'Create a multiple-choice quiz of 10 questions on the topic of data collection for my research methods class for undergraduate business students'.

4.7.2. Facilitate Research

Prompt engineering is useful for researchers to summarise the literature, generate research questions, assist in writing, and explore new ideas, thereby supporting the research process and enhancing research and publication productivity (Giray, 2023; Qian, 2025). Example: 'Generate a list of potential research questions related to the responsible use of AI'.

4.7.3. Interactive Learning Tools for Student Feedback

Prompt engineering is useful for lecturers to develop interactive learning tools, such as chatbots and virtual tutors, that provide an engaging learning experience for students, support them, and provide personalised feedback (Ali et al., 2023; Serra & Oliveira, 2025).

5. CONCLUSION

With the rapid 'AI boom' across all sectors, prompt engineering is emerging not just as a technical skill but also as a creative one, enabling more natural interactions between humans and machines and bridging the gap between human intent and machine understanding. By developing the skill of crafting contextually rich prompts, educators, researchers, and practitioners can harness the capabilities of Gen AI models, such as LLMs. These models, when prompted skilfully, can yield far-fetched, coherent, and contextually relevant outputs that amplify education and research and enhance student learning experiences.

In this chapter, we lay the foundations of prompt engineering, highlighting its applications in academia and featuring the significance of well-engineered prompts on the quality and relevance of AI-generated content. Driven by ongoing AI advances and their integration into practically all domains, the role of prompt engineering will undoubtedly expand. By being proficient in prompt engineering, we can harness the power of AI to drive innovation, learning, and growth.

REFERENCES

Adamopoulou, E., & Moussiades, L. (2020). An overview of chatbot technology. In I. Maglogiannis, L. Iliadis, & E. Pimenidis (Eds.), *Artificial intelligence applications and innovations* (IFIP Advances in Information and Communication Technology, Vol. 584, pp. 373–383). Springer. https://doi.org/10.1007/978-3-030-49186-4_31

AlAfnan, M. A. (2025). Technical report writing efficiency using AI-powered tools: Opportunities, challenges, and future directions. *Journal of Artificial Intelligence and Technology*, *5*, 270–277.

Ali, F., Choy, D., Divaharan, S., Tay, H. Y., & Chen, W. (2023). Supporting self-directed learning and self-assessment using TeacherGAIA, a generative

AI chatbot application: Learning approaches and prompt engineering. *Learning: Research and Practice*, 9(2), 135–147.

Alizadeh, M., Kubli, M., Samei, Z., Dehghani, S., Zahedivafa, M., Bermeo, J. D., Korobeynikova, M., & Gilardi, F. (2025). Open-source LLMs for text annotation: A practical guide for model setting and fine-tuning. *Journal of Computational Social Science*, *8*(1), 17.

Arora, S., Narayan, A., Chen, M. F., Orr, L., Guha, N., Bhatia, K., Chami, I., Sala, F., & Ré, C. (2022). Ask me anything: A simple strategy for prompting language models. *arXiv preprint arXiv:2210.02441*.

Arugula, B. (2025). Prompt engineering for LLMs: Real-world applications in banking and ecommerce. *International Journal of Artificial Intelligence, Data Science, and Machine Learning*, 6(1), 115–123.

Banh, L., & Strobel, G. (2023). Generative artificial intelligence. *Electronic Markets*, *33*(1), Article 63. https://doi.org/10.1007/s12525-023-00680-1

Boon-Itt, S., & Skunkan, Y. (2020). Public perception of the COVID-19 pandemic on Twitter: Sentiment analysis and topic modeling study. *JMIR Public Health and Surveillance*, 6(4), e21978.

Brown, T. B., Mann, B., Ryder, N., Subbiah, M., Kaplan, J. D., Dhariwal, P., Neelakantan, A., Shyam, P., Sastry, G., Askell, A., Agarwal, S., Herbert-Voss, A., Krueger, G., Henighan, T., Child, R., Ramesh, A., Ziegler, D. M., Wu, J., Winter, C., … Amodei, D. (2020). Language models are few-shot learners. *Advances in Neural Information Processing Systems*, *33*, 1877–1901.

Canyakan, S. (2025). Comparative accuracy of AI-based plagiarism detection tools: An enhanced systematic review. *Journal of AI, Humanities and New Ethics*, *1*(1), 5–18.

Chandra, S., Shirish, A., & Srivastava, S. C. (2022). To be or not to be … human? Theorising the role of human-like competencies in conversational artificial intelligence agents. *Journal of Management Information Systems*, *39*(4), 969–1005.

Chkirbene, Z., Hamila, R., Gouissem, A., & Devrim, U. (2024). *Large language models (LLM) in industry: A survey of applications, challenges, and trends* [Conference paper]. In 2024 IEEE 21st international conference on smart communities: Improving quality of life using AI, robotics and IoT (HONET) (pp. 229–234). IEEE.

Cohan, A., Dernoncourt, F., Kim, D. S., Bui, T., Kim, S., Chang, W., & Goharian, N. (2018). *A discourse-aware attention model for abstractive summarisation of long documents* [Short paper]. In Proceedings of the 2018 conference of the North American chapter of the Association for Computational Linguistics: Human Language technologies (Vol. 2, pp. 615–621). ACL.

Devlin, J., Chang, M.-W., Lee, K., & Toutanova, K. (2019). *BERT: Pretraining of deep bidirectional transformers for language understanding* [Long and short papers]. In Proceedings of the 2019 conference of the North American chapter of the Association for Computational Linguistics: Human Language Technologies (Vol. 1, pp. 4171–4186). ACL.

Duan, H., Wei, J., Wang, C., Liu, H., Fang, Y., Zhang, S., Lin, D., & Chen, K. (2024). *BotChat: Evaluating LLMs' capabilities of having multi-turn dialogues.* In Findings of the Association for Computational Linguistics (NAACL 2024, pp. 3184–3200). ACL.

Eager, B., & Brunton, R. (2023). Prompting higher education towards AI-augmented teaching and learning practice. *Journal of University Teaching and Learning Practice*, *20*(5), 1–19.

Eymann, V., Lachmann, T., & Czernochowski, D. (2025). When ChatGPT writes your research proposal: Scientific creativity in the age of generative AI. *Journal of Intelligence*, *13*(5), 55.

Gatys, L. A., Ecker, A. S., & Bethge, M. (2016). *Image style transfer using convolutional neural networks* [Conference paper]. Proceedings of the IEEE conference on computer vision and pattern recognition (pp. 2414–2423). IEEE.

Giatsoglou, M., Vozalis, M. G., Diamantaras, K., Vakali, A., Sarigiannidis, G., & Chatzisavvas, K. C. (2017). Sentiment analysis leveraging emotions and word embeddings. *Expert Systems with Applications*, *69*, 214–224.

Giray, L. (2023). Prompt engineering with ChatGPT: A guide for academic writers. *Annals of Biomedical Engineering*, *51*(12), 2629–2633.

Goodfellow, I., Bengio, Y., Courville, A., & Bengio, Y. (2016). *Deep learning* (Vol. 1). MIT Press.

Howard, J., & Ruder, S. (2018). Universal language model fine-tuning for text classification. In I. Gurevych & Y. Miyao (Eds.), *Proceedings of the 56th Annual Meeting of the Association for Computational Linguistics (Volume 1: Long Papers)* (pp. 328–339). Association for Computational Linguistics. https://doi.org/10.18653/v1/P18-1031

Jasmine, K. S. (2024). Unlocking the power of prompt engineering: Diverse applications and case studies. In R. C. Sharma & A. Bozkurt (Eds.), *Transforming education with generative AI: Prompt engineering and synthetic content creation* (pp. 411–432). IGI Global.

Jeong, C. (2024). Fine-tuning and utilisation methods of domain-specific LLMs. arXiv preprint arXiv:2401.02981.

Jim, J. R., Talukder, M. A. R., Malakar, P., Kabir, M. M., Nur, K., & Mridha, M. F. (2024). Recent advancements and challenges of NLP-based sentiment analysis: A state-of-the-art review. *Natural Language Processing Journal*, 6, 100059.

LeCun, Y., Bengio, Y., & Hinton, G. (2015). Deep learning. *Nature*, *521*(7553), 436–444.

Liu, Y., Ott, M., Goyal, N., Du, J., Joshi, M., Chen, D., Levy, O., Lewis, M., Zettlemoyer, L., & Stoyanov, V. (2019). RoBERTa: A robustly optimised BERT pretraining approach. *arXiv preprint arXiv:1907.11692.*

Mäntylä, M. V., Graziotin, D., & Kuutila, M. (2018). The evolution of sentiment analysis—A review of research topics, venues, and top-cited papers. *Computer Science Review*, 27, 16–32.

Marvin, G., Hellen, N., Jjingo, D., & Nakatumba-Nabende, J. (2023). Prompt engineering in large language models. In *International Conference on Data Intelligence and Cognitive Informatics* (pp. 387–402). Springer Nature Singapore. https://doi.org/10.1007/978-981-99-6741-5_30

Mikolov, T., Chen, K., Corrado, G., & Dean, J. (2013). Efficient estimation of word representations in vector space. *arXiv preprint arXiv:1301.3781.*

Minaee, S., Kalchbrenner, N., Cambria, E., Nikzad, N., Chenaghlu, M., & Gao, J. (2021). Deep learning-based text classification: A comprehensive review. *ACM Computing Surveys (CSUR)*, *54*(3), 1–40.

Mitchell, T. M. (1997). Does machine learning really work? *AI Magazine*, *18*(3), 11–20.

Mondal, A. S., Zhu, Y., Bhagat, K. K., & Giacaman, N. (2024). Analysing user reviews of interactive educational apps: A sentiment analysis approach. *Interactive Learning Environments*, *32*(1), 355–372.

Norouzi, K., Ghodsi, A., Argani, P., Andi, P. A., & Hassani, H. (2025). Innovative artificial intelligence tools: Exploring the future of healthcare through IBM Watson's potential applications. In T. A. Nguyen (Ed.), *Sensor networks for smart hospitals* (pp. 573–588). Elsevier.

Oord, A. v. d., Dieleman, S., Zen, H., Simonyan, K., Vinyals, O., Graves, A., Kalchbrenner, N., Senior, A., & Kavukcuoglu, K. (2016). WaveNet: A generative model for raw audio. *arXiv preprint arXiv:1609.03499.*

Payne, C. (2019, April 25). *MuseNet* [OpenAI Blog]. Retrieved March 19, from https://openai.com/index/musenet/

Pennington, J., Socher, R., & Manning, C. D. (2014). GloVe: Global vectors for word representation. In A. Moschitti, B. Pang, & W. Daelemans (Eds.), *Proceedings of the 2014 Conference on Empirical Methods in Natural Language Processing (EMNLP)* (pp. 1532–1543). Association for Computational Linguistics. https://doi.org/10.3115/v1/D14-1162

Qian, Y. (2025). Prompt engineering in education: A systematic review of approaches and educational applications. *Journal of Educational Computing Research*, *63*(7–8), 1782–1818.

Ramesh, A., Pavlov, M., Goh, G., Gray, S., Voss, C., Radford, A., Chen, M., & Sutskever, I. (2021). Zero-shot text-to-image generation. *Proceedings of Machine Learning Research*, *139*, 8821–8831.

Ray, P. P. (2023). ChatGPT: A comprehensive review on background, applications, key challenges, bias, ethics, limitations and future scope. *Internet of Things and Cyber-physical Systems*, *3*, 121–154.

Reynolds, L., & McDonell, K. (2021). Prompt programming for large language models: Beyond the few-shot paradigm. In *Extended Abstracts of the 2021 CHI Conference on Human Factors in Computing Systems* (pp. 1–7). Association for Computing Machinery. https://doi.org/10.1145/3411763.3451760

Russell, S., & Norvig, P. (2010). *Artificial intelligence: A modern approach* (3rd ed.). Prentice-Hall.

Serra, P., & Oliveira, Â. (2025). AI-powered prompt engineering for education 4.0: Transforming digital resources into engaging learning experiences. *Education Sciences*, *15*(12), 1640.

Stiennon, N., Ouyang, L., Wu, J., Ziegler, D., Lowe, R., Voss, C., Radford, A., Amodei, D., & Christiano, P. F. (2020). Learning to summarise with human feedback. *Advances in Neural Information Processing Systems*, *33*, 3008–3021.

Sun, C., Qiu, X., Xu, Y., & Huang, X. (2019). How to fine-tune BERT for text classification? In *China National Conference on Chinese Computational Linguistics* (pp. 194–206). Springer International Publishing. https://doi.org/10.1007/978-3-030-32381-3_17

Sutton, R. S., & Barto, A. G. (1998). *Reinforcement learning: An introduction* (Vol. 1). MIT Press.

Vaswani, A., Shazeer, N., Parmar, N., Uszkoreit, J., Jones, L., Gomez, A. N., Kaiser, Ł., & Polosukhin, I. (2017). Attention is all you need. In *Advances in Neural Information Processing Systems* (Vol. 30, pp. 5998–6008). https://doi.org/10.48550/arXiv.1706.03762

von Ahn, L. (2013). Duolingo: Learn a language for free while helping to translate the web. In J. Kim, J. Nichols, & P. Szekely (Eds.), *Proceedings of the 2013 International Conference on Intelligent User Interfaces* (pp. 1–2). Association for Computing Machinery.

Walton, Z. (2020). *AI Dungeon: A text adventure game powered by GPT-3* [Latitude Blog]. Retrieved March 19, from https://latitude.io/news/ai-dungeon

Wolf, T., Debut, L., Sanh, V., Chaumond, J., Delangue, C., Moi, A., Cistac, P., Rault, T., Louf, R., Funtowicz, M., Davison, J., Shleifer, S., von Platen, P., Ma, C., Jernite, Y., Plu, J., Xu, C., Le Scao, T., Gugger, S., ..., Rush, A. (2020). *Transformers: State-of-the-art natural language processing* [Conference paper]. In Proceedings of the 2020 conference on empirical methods in natural language processing: System demonstrations (pp. 38–45). ACL.

Xie, T., Kuang, Y., Tang, Y., Liao, J., & Yang, Y. (2025). Using LLM-supported lecture summarisation system to improve knowledge recall and student satisfaction. *Expert Systems with Applications, 269*, 126371.

Yan, H., Zhang, H., Liu, L., Zhou, D., Xu, X., Zhang, Z., & Yan, S. (2022). Toward intelligent design: An AI-based fashion designer using generative adversarial networks aided by sketch and rendering generators. *IEEE Transactions on Multimedia, 25*, 2323–2338.

2

CRAFTING EFFECTIVE PROMPTS: THINKING WITH MACHINES NOT JUST TALKING TO THEM

ABSTRACT

This chapter develops a conceptual and practical foundation for crafting effective prompts in the context of generative artificial intelligence (Gen AI) use in academia. Moving beyond the view of prompts as simple instructions, the chapter positions prompting as a form of cognitive framing that shapes how large language models (LLMs) interpret tasks, generate outputs, and support scholarly work. It introduces different types of prompts – informational, instructional, creative, and conversational – and demonstrates how each aligns with distinct academic purposes such as knowledge retrieval, teaching design, research ideation, and human–AI interaction. Drawing on emerging research in prompt engineering and human–AI interaction, the chapter highlights how specificity, context, and structure influence output quality. It further examines the role of iterative prompting, showing how refinement, constraint and dialogic engagement can transform AI from a passive tool into an active thinking partner. At the same time, the chapter critically engages with the limitations of Gen AI, including risks of superficial coherence and epistemic unreliability.

Keywords: Prompt engineering; generative AI; large language model; academic writing; human–AI interaction; iterative prompting; cognitive framing

Chapter Goal: Provide an approach to writing initial prompts

1. INTRODUCTION

For many academics, the first encounter with an LLM is both exciting and strangely disappointing.

You open the interface of a system such as ChatGPT or Google Gemini and type a simple request. For example,

Explain institutional theory.

Within seconds, a response appears. It is polished, well structured, fluent, confident, and grammatically impeccable. At first glance, the answer appears impressive. The system seems to understand the topic and provides an explanation that is broadly accurate.

And then comes quiet disappointment.

It is correct but generic.

Comprehensive but unsurprising.

It is coherent but predictable. Smooth but shallow.

That moment is important. At this moment, many scholars reach a quiet conclusion: perhaps Gen AI is impressive, but not particularly useful for serious intellectual work.

This conclusion, however, usually reflects a misunderstanding of how LLMs operate. The problem is rarely the model itself. Instead, it lies in the way we interact with it. This reveals something fundamental: LLMs do not respond to curiosity. They respond to instruction. It's like a machine you programme with words (Mollick, 2023).

LLMs do not simply respond to questions in the same way that humans do. Rather, they generate text based on patterns learned from vast collections of written material. Their responses are shaped heavily by the context and instructions embedded within the prompt. In other words, the quality of the output depends on the quality of the input.

If we treat them like search engines, they disappoint us. If we treat them like junior collaborators who require careful direction, they become astonishingly capable.

The difference lies in the prompt. That is why prompting has become such a central concept in the use of Gen AI. A prompt is not merely a question. It is a structured instruction that guides the model toward a particular type of response.

But not in the superficial way the Internet suggests.

Prompting is not about inserting magic phrases like 'act as an expert' or 'think step by step'. Those can help, as research by Wei at al. (2022) and Kojima et al. (2022) demonstrates, but they are not the essence of the craft.

The real shift is epistemic.

The importance of prompts becomes clear when researchers introduce powerful language models such as GPT-3. The influential paper describing CGT-3 demonstrated that the behaviour of a language model could change dramatically depending on how a task was framed within the prompt (Brown et al., 2020). Instead of retraining models for every task, researchers discovered that they could achieve different behaviours simply by changing the prompt itself.

This discovery led to the emergence of a new practice known as prompt engineering. Although the term may sound technical, its essence is quite intuitive.

When we prompt an LLM, we're not asking for information. We are shipping a probability space.

Models such as those developed by OpenAI (ChatGPT) are trained to predict the next word based on patterns from vast text corpora (Brown et al., 2020). They do not 'know' things in the human sense. They estimate what is likely to come next in a given context.

The prompt is that context.

A vague prompt creates a wide field of possibilities. The model selects the safest, most statistically common continuation. That is why early interactions often feel bland. A precise prompt narrows the field. It signals depth, stance, structure, and expectation. It reduces ambiguity. Therefore, crafting a good prompt is akin to giving the AI a clear set of instructions – much like writing a lesson plan or research brief (Mollick, 2023). In other words, good prompting is less about eloquence and more about intellectual clarity.

And this is where academies have an advantage – if they realise it.

We already design arguments carefully.

We already structured research questions deliberately.

We already specify methods precisely.

Prompt engineering is not foreign to scholarly thinking. It is an extension of it.

The challenge is that we instinctively under-specify when we interact with machines. We assume they will infer our intent… they cannot.

They infer statistical regularities, not unspoken nuance. Moreover, LLMs are found to be recognising user intentions and sentiments better by analysing context information present in the prompt or query (Wei et al., 2022).

Once this is understood, prompting becomes less mysterious and more methodological. It involves understanding how LLMs interpret instructions and how prompts can structure intellectual tasks.

This chapter explores how academics can craft effective prompts by understanding the logic behind them. Rather than presenting a list of technical shortcuts, the chapter develops a conceptual approach to promoting that aligns with the habits of scholarly thinking.

2. UNDERSTANDING HOW LLMs WORK

Before exploring how to craft effective prompts, it is helpful to understand, at least at a conceptual level, how LLMs generate responses.

Systems such as ChatGPT and Claude AI are based on a machine learning architecture known as the transformer model. Introduced by Vaswani et al. (2017), transformer models revolutionised natural language processing by enabling computers to analyse relationships between words within large bodies of text.

These models are trained on enormous datasets that include books, academic articles, websites, and other written materials. During training, the model learns statistical relationships between words and phrases. For example, it learns that the phrase 'institutional isomorphism' frequently appears alongside discussions of organisational sociology and the work of DiMaggio and Powell (1983).

Importantly, however, the model does not store knowledge in the same way that humans do. Instead, it learns patterns that allow it to predict the most probable next work in a sequence of text.

When a user enters a prompt, the model analyses the prompt as context and then begins generating text one token at a time, predicting each subsequent word based on probabilities derived from its training.

This process means that the model's output is not retrieved from a database. It is generated dynamically based on the prompt.

As a result, the same model can produce dramatically different responses depending on how a prompt is written. A vague prompt may produce a generic response, while a carefully structured prompt can guide the model toward more focused explanations.

Think of prompt engineering as a new faculty skill, one that is being incorporated into teaching frameworks. Lee and Palmer (2025) argue that prompt engineering should be viewed as a 'steering mechanism' – a skill that educators can learn and teach. It is not about tricks; it is about placing constraints and signals in your prompt so that AI's statistical tendencies align with your goals. The user's information need is like an iceberg (Fig. 9). The visible tip of this iceberg is the direct prompt, which includes request, reference, format, and framing (Budiu et al., 2023). While the submerged layers are the

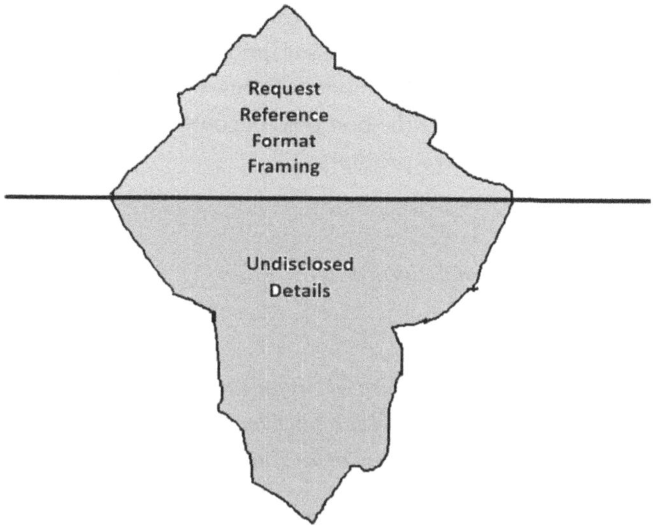

Fig. 9. The Iceberg Model of AI Prompts.

critical elements that give the prompt its true shape and direction. The more of these submerged layers that are revealed in the prompt, the more effective the AI can be in meeting the user's information need. Working on the visible part of the iceberg and providing requests, references, formats, and framing can be relatively straightforward for many of us. However, determining the right framing for the prompt can be tricky, as uncovering all the contextual information can take a lot of effort, and also providing too many unnecessary details can sidetrack the LLM.

Recent research has shown that even subtle changes in prompts can significantly affect the performance of language models (Liu et al., 2023). Techniques such as chain-of thought prompting (we will discuss in the section below), which encourage models to articulate intermediate reasoning steps, have been shown to improve performance on complex reasoning tasks (Wei et al., 2022).

3. PROMPTS AS INTELLECTUAL INSTRUCTIONS

One useful way to think about prompts is to treat them as intellectual instructions rather than questions.

In traditional computing systems, instructions take the form of explicit commands written in programming language. With LLMs, however, instructions are written in natural language.

This difference is important. Because prompts are expressed in natural language, they can incorporate context, assumptions, and expectations in ways that resemble ordinary scholarly communications. It can involve words, phrases, formats, and symbols to get the best possible outcome (Johnmaeda, 2023).

Consider the following two prompts:

Prompt A:

> *Explain organisational culture.*

Prompt B:

> *Provide a concise explanation of organisational culture based on Edgar Schein's three-level model. The explanation should be suitable for undergraduate business students.*

The first prompt leaves many aspects of the task undefined. The model must decide which theoretical perspective to use, how detailed the explanation should be, and who the audience might be.

The second prompt, by contrast, provides clear instructions. It specifies the theoretical framework, the level of explanations and the intended audience.

As a result, the second prompt is more likely to produce a useful response.

Let's take another example:

A vague prompt like 'discuss global ethics' yields a broad paragraph that skims the surface.

A refined prompt, by contrast, might be: 'you are a business ethics professor explaining global business ethics to MBA students. In 400 words, compare deontological and consequentialist approaches, using examples from real corporations. End by posing a class discussion question.'

This rich prompt is essentially a mini assignment. It specifies the role (business ethics professor), the audience (MBA students), the task (compare theories), length (400 words), content focus (examples from corporations), and even output form (includes a discussion question). The AI's answer will be on-target: structured and context-rich. Lee and Palmer (2025) suggest that prompts aligned with clear educational goals produce much higher-quality content.

4. THE CORE COMPONENTS OF EFFECTIVE PROMPTS: THE STAR PROMPT FRAMEWORK

A helpful way to remember key prompt elements is the STAR framework:

- S – *Set the stage*: Define context and role (e.g., 'you are a researcher…').

- T – *Task*: Use specific verbs (e.g., explain, compare, generate) to define the action.
- A – *Audience*: Indicate who will 'receive' the answer (e.g., students, managers, peers).
- R – *Restrictions/format*: State any limits (e.g., word count, bullet points, tone) (Cook, 2023).

For example, consider instructing the model to create quiz questions:

> *you are an MBA instructor. Generate three case-based quiz questions about ethical decision-making. Each question should describe a brief scenario and ask students to apply utilitarianism. Use bullet points.*

This prompt sets a scenario (instructor's role), audience (MBA students) and clear output format (bullet questions). The AI then produces relevant, detailed prompts. Using STAR principles transforms a vague request into a precise blueprint.

Being specific and providing more details not only helps you in understanding your prompt better but also generates responses with lesser errors.

5. TYPES OF PROMPTS AND THEIR SIGNIFICANCE

Prompts can be designed for many different purposes. In academic contexts, four broad categories are particularly useful.

5.1. Informational Prompts

Informational prompts are designed to retrieve explanations or definitions.

Example:

> *Explain the difference between classical and operant conditioning.*

These prompts are valuable for clarifying concepts or generating introductory explanations. However, because language models generate text probabilistically, informational responses should always be verified against authoritative sources like experts, published articles, etc.

5.2. Creative Prompts

Creative prompts encourage the model to generate imaginative content. They can often be introduced in the most simplistic way as tools for generating stories, poems, or artistic content. While this description is not incorrect, it significantly underestimates their relevance, especially in academic contexts.

At a deeper level, creative prompts enable something far more important: they allow users to explore possibility spaces, to imagine what could exist, rather than simply retrieve what already does.

Example:

> *Write a short story about a dragon who loves gardening.*

At first glance, this may appear trivial or unrelated to academic work. However, what the model is doing here is cognitively significant. It is combining two unrelated domains – mythical creatures and domestic horticulture – into a coherent narrative. This reflects a fundamental mechanism of creativity: the recombination of existing concepts into novel configurations (Boden, 2004).

LLMs are particularly adept at this form of recombination because they have been trained on vast and diverse textual corpora. As a result, they can generate unexpected but plausible connections between ideas. For scholars, this capability becomes especially valuable when dealing with ill-defined problems, early-stage research ideas, or interdisciplinary questions. Academic inquiry does not always begin with clear hypotheses. Often, it begins with ambiguity, curiosity, and the need to explore alternative ways of framing a problem.

Creative prompts can support this phase of inquiry and be core to some academic disciplines, like music, fashion, etc. Scholars can sometimes use creative prompts to explore metaphors, thought experiments, or speculative scenarios that stimulate new lines of enquiry. For instance, a researcher studying organisational behaviour might use a creative prompt such as:

> *Imagine an organisation where all decision-making is guided by AI rather than human managers. What new forms of leadership might emerge?*

This is not a request for factual information. Instead, it is a thought experiment. The goal is to generate possibilities that can later be examined critically. In this sense, creative prompts function as tools for conceptual exploration.

They are particularly useful in disciplines where imagination plays a central role, such as design, architecture, media studies, or the creative arts.

But their relevance extends far beyond these fields. Even in traditionally analytical disciplines, creative prompts can help scholars:

- Generate metaphors to explain complex theories.
- Explore alternative conceptual frameworks.
- Identify unconventional research questions.
- Test the boundaries of existing assumptions.

Another important use of creative prompting lies in the development of pedagogical material. Educators can use such prompts to create engaging scenarios that help students understand abstract concepts.

For example:

> *Create a fictional scenario that illustrates the tension between profit maximisation and social responsibility in a multinational corporation.*

Here, creativity serves a pedagogical purpose. It transforms abstract theory into a narrative that students can relate to and analyse.

However, it is important to recognise the limitations of creative prompts. While they generate novel ideas, these ideas are not inherently valid or rigorous. They must be evaluated, refined, and situated within existing scholarly frameworks.

In other words, creative prompts are not a substitute for academic reasoning; rather, they are tools for expanding the horizon of thought.

5.3. Instructional Prompt

Instructional prompts represent a different mode of interaction with Gen AI systems. Instead of exploring possibilities, they focus on procedural clarity by breaking down complex tasks into structured steps.

A typical example might be:

> *Explain how to set up a virtual machine using VMware.*

At a surface level, this appears to be a straightforward request for instructions. However, what makes instructional prompting powerful is the way it translates implicit knowledge into explicit guidance.

Many academic and professional tasks involve forms of tacit knowledge – skills that experts perform intuitively but may find difficult to articulate.

Instructional prompts encourage the model to externalise this knowledge in a structured form. Such prompts are useful for learning technical procedures or explaining complex processes.

For instance, a more refined instructional prompt might be:

> *Provide a step-by-step guide to setting up a virtual machine using VMware for a beginner with no prior experience. Include common errors and how to avoid them.*

This version improves the output in several ways. It specifies the audience, the level of expertise, and the need to anticipate potential challenges. As a result, the generated response is more likely to be practical and accessible.

In academic contexts, instructional prompts can support a wide range of activities. They can assist in clarifying research methods:

> *Explain how to conduct a thematic analysis of qualitative data, including coding and theme development.*

They can help structure academic writing processes:

> *Provide a step-by-step approach to writing a literature review in organisational behaviour.*

They can also support teaching by generating structured explanations of complex procedures.

What makes instructional prompts particularly valuable is their ability to bridge the gap between knowledge and practice. While informational prompts explain concepts, instructional prompts show how those concepts are applied.

However, there are important considerations when using instructional prompts.

First, AI-generated instructions are not guaranteed to be accurate or complete. Users must verify the steps, particularly when dealing with technical or high-stakes tasks. Second, overly generic prompts can lead to superficial instructions. Without sufficient context, the model may produce steps that are technically correct but not tailored to the user's needs.

To improve the effectiveness of instructional prompts, it is helpful to:

- Specify the level of expertise of the intended audience.
- Indicate the context in which the task is being performed.
- Request structured outputs (e.g., numbered steps).
- Include constraints or desired outcomes.

When designed thoughtfully, instructional prompts can transform Gen AI into a procedural guide, supporting both learning and application.

5.4. Conversational Prompts

While informational and instructional prompts tend to be task-oriented, conversational prompts encourage dialogue. They are in a more dynamic and exploratory mode of interaction.

Example:

> *What are the main arguments for and against the use of social media in higher education?*

At first glance, this appears similar to an informational prompt. However, the key difference lies in what happens next.

Conversational prompting is not a single exchange. It is an ongoing dialogue in which each response becomes the basis for further questioning. It allows researchers to explore topics iteratively, refining questions as the dialogue unfolds.

For example, a researcher might begin with the prompt above and then continue:

> *Which of these arguments are most relevant for developing countries?*

Followed by:

> *How might these concerns differ across disciplines?*

Through this sequence, the interaction evolves into a dialogic process. The user is not simply retrieving information but actively shaping the direction of inquiry.

This approach aligns closely with how academic thinking often develops. Scholars rarely arrive at insights through isolated questions. Instead, they refine their understanding through iterative questioning, discussion, and reflection.

Conversational prompts allow Gen AI systems to participate in this process. They are particularly valuable in situations where the problem is not fully defined. For example:

- Exploring a new research area.
- Testing preliminary ideas.

- Examining multiple perspectives on a topic.
- Identifying gaps or tensions in existing knowledge.

Educational research highlights the importance of dialogue in learning, suggesting that knowledge is constructed through interaction rather than passive reception (Mercer & Littleton, 2007). Conversational prompting reflects this principle by enabling users to engage actively with generated content.

However, the effectiveness of conversational prompts depends heavily on the user's ability to guide the dialogue. Without direction, the interaction may remain superficial.

To deepen the conversation, users can:

- Ask follow-up questions that probe assumptions.
- Request clarification or elaboration.
- Introduce alternative perspectives.
- Challenge the response critically.

For example:

> *That explanation focuses on benefits. What are the potential ethical risks?*

Such prompts encourage the model to move beyond initial responses and engage with more complex aspects of the topic.

In this sense, conversational prompting transforms the AI system into a thinking partner, not in the sense of possessing independent understanding, but in its ability to generate responses that stimulate further reflection.

6. PROMPTING TECHNIQUES

Prompt engineering focuses on designing prompts that improve reliability and performance across different tasks. While earlier examples illustrated basic capabilities, this section introduces more advanced prompting techniques that enable more complex behaviour.

6.1. Zero-shot Prompting in Academic Work

Modern LLMs today, such as GPT-3.5 Turbo, GPT-4, and Claude 3, are trained on large datasets and instruction-tuned to follow natural language commands. This allows them to perform some tasks in a zero-shot manner, meaning no examples or demonstrations are included in the prompt. The zero-shot prompt directly instructs the model to perform a task without any additional examples to steer it (Wei et al., 2022). Zero-shot prompting means giving no examples. For example:

> *Classify the following abstract as qualitative, quantitative, or mixed methods.*

This works because the model has been trained on enough academic text to recognise patterns. Zero-shot works well for:

- Concept explanations.
- Basic classification.
- Summarisation.
- Brainstorming.

Here, the model successfully performed sentiment classification without any examples. This capability is largely attributed to instruction tuning, which fine-tunes models on datasets framed as natural language instructions (Wei et al., 2022). In addition, reinforcement learning from human feedback (RLHF) is commonly used to align model outputs with human preferences – an approach that underpins systems such as ChatGPT.

It struggles with:

- Complex reasoning.
- Precise formatting.
- Novel tasks.
- Edge-case conceptual distinctions.

When zero-shot prompting fails, a common remedy is to include examples in the prompt. This leads to few-shot prompting, discussed next.

6.2. Few-Shot Prompting for Academic Style Conditioning

Although LLMs exhibit strong zero-shot performance on many tasks, more complex problems often benefit from few-shot prompting where demonstrations are provided directly in the prompt. These demonstrations condition the model through in-context learning, guiding its behaviour without updating model parameters.

According to Touvron et al. (2023), few-shot properties first appeared when models were scaled to a sufficient size (Kaplan et al., 2020).

Few-shot prompting means providing examples. This is extremely useful for:

- Conditioning tone.
- Matching writing style.
- Enforcing labelling conventions.
- Generating structured outputs.

Example for reviewer responses:

Prompt:

Reviewer comment:	'The theoretical contribution is unclear.'
Author response:	'Thank you for this insightful comment. We have clarified our theoretical contribution in section 4 by....'
Reviewer comment:	'The sample size appears limited.'
Author response:	'We appreciate this observation. While the sample size is modest, it aligns with...'
Reviewer comment:	'The hypotheses lack clarity.'
Author response:	'The model will continue the patterned politeness and structure.'

You are teaching it rhetorical convention. Few-shot prompting is particularly powerful in academia because academic writing follows stable rhetorical norms. Few-shot prompting is effective for many tasks but remains unreliable for problems that require multi-step reasoning.

6.3. Chain-of-Thought Prompting for Scholarly Reasoning

While it is well-known that outcomes produced by LLMs are far from perfect, inaccuracies in high-stake fields like education and medicine can lead to more severe consequences as compared to other fields (Correia et al., 2025). Direct prompts can often lead to such inaccuracies; thus, for complex tasks – especially theory integration – instructing the model through sophisticated prompts can be very effective. Moreover, LLMs tend to skip critical reasoning steps and provide answers that lack transparency (Wei et al., 2022). Prompts that can be used to reason step-by-step can make the whole process more transparent and accessible to improve performance. Chain-of-thought prompting is one such advanced prompting technique that guides LLMs to produce results which are detailed based on step-by-step reasoning (Zhang et al., 2022). Instead of:

> *Does institutional theory support stakeholder governance?*

Try:

> *Analyse whether institutional theory support stakeholder governance. First, summarise the core assumptions of institutional theory. Second, outline the principles of stakeholder governance. Third, evaluate points of alignment and tension. Conclude with a reasoned position.*

You are scaffolding reasoning.
You are externalising the intellectual process.
This is profoundly useful for:

- Theory comparison.
- Argument development.
- Literature synthesis.
- Conceptual clarification.

By mimicking the human 'think aloud process', chain-of-thought guides the LLMs to break down complex problems into smaller, manageable chunks, leading to more coherent and accurate outcomes.

7. REFLECTIVE PAUSE

Before proceeding further, consider:

- How do you currently write prompts?
- Are you specifying output architecture?
- Are you distinguishing between task and context?
- Are you iterating or accepting first drafts?

Most academics do not fail at prompting because they lack intelligence, but because they do not externalise their intellectual standards into the prompt.

We are not limited by what the model 'knows'.

We are limited by how clearly we articulate what we wanted to do. This has profound implications for academics.

And yet, clarity is difficult.

Many early-career academics feel that their prompts must sound sophisticated. They tried to craft elaborate instructions filled with jargon. Ironically, this often reduces quality.

LLMs respond better to structured thinking than ornamental language.

Instead of asking:

> *Provide a comprehensive and critically reflexive exposition of institutional contradictions in contemporary ESG governance paradigms....*

Try:

> *Explain the main intentions in ESG governance.*
>
> *First describe the shareholder perspective.*
>
> *Then describe the stakeholder perspective.*
>
> *Then explain why they conflict.*

It's just not about something clever. It is about sequencing cognition. Prompting, then, is less casting a spell and more site designing of a syllabus.

You decide:

What comes first.

What follows.

What should be compared.

What should be constrained.

This is why prompting improves with experience. Not because one memorises techniques, like because one begins to see how structure shapes output.

There is another misconception worth confronting.

Many academics believe that the goal of prompting is to obtain the 'perfect' output in one attempt. This is really how serious work happens.

Scholarly writing is iterative. We draft, refine, critique, and redraft. Prompting should follow the same pattern or rhythm.

An effective workflow might look like this:

You ask the model to draft an abstract.

Then you ask it to critique that abstract for vagueness.

Then you ask it to strengthen the contribution statement.

Then you ask it to identify hidden assumptions.

Each prompt builds up on the previous one.

Research on self-consistency prompting (Wang et al., 2022) shows that generating multiple reasoning paths improves reliability. In practice, this means one should treat outputs as provisional – as intellectual materials to sculpt, not finished products to submit.

This is especially important because, as Bender et al. (2021) caution, these models can produce fluent nonsense. They may fabricate citations. They may overstate certainty.

Fluency is not validity. Prompting, therefore, requires epistemic discipline.

Used passively, it encourages cognitive offloading – the tendency to outsource thinking to external systems (Risko & Gilbert, 2016). Used activity, it sharpens thinking by exposing gaps, inconsistencies, and unexamined assumptions.

The difference lies in posture.

If you ask, 'write this for me', you relinquish authorship.

If you ask, 'where is my reasoning weak?' you deepen authorship.

That's here from delegation to orchestration is the heart of effective prompt engineering for academics.

The remainder of this chapter will not offer a list of clever tricks. Instead, it will develop a mental model for designing prompts that produce meaningful, structured, and reliable intellectual output. We will examine how to specify tasks precisely, how to guide reasoning without suffocating creativity, how to simulate peer review through prompting, and how to avoid the subtle traps the generative systems create.

Prompting is not about talking to machines … it is about learning how to think with them!

If prompting is about shaping how a model responds, the next logical question is simple: what exactly should we include in a prompt to guide that response effectively?

The answer is surprisingly similar to how scholars design research questions. A well-designed research question clarifies the phenomenon, situates the inquiry, specifies the perspective, and often signals the methodological approach. Prompts operate in a comparable way. They work best when they clearly establish context, task, expectation, and constraints. Without these elements, a language model must rely on generic statistical associations, which often result in broad but shallow responses.

Consider a familiar academic activity: preparing a lecture.

A lecturer experimenting with Gen AI might write a prompt such as:

> *Explain institutional theory to MBA students.*
>
> *The response will likely include definitions, references to foundational scholars such as Meyer and Rowan or DiMaggio and Powell, and a brief discussion of institutional isomorphism. None of this is incorrect, yet the explanation may still feel unhelpful for teaching. It lacks pedagogical framing, illustrative examples, and the conceptual progression needed for classroom engagement.*

Now compare this with a more deliberately constructed prompt:

> *I am preparing a lecture on institutional theory for MBA students who have little background in sociology.*
>
> *Explain institutional theory in three stages: first introduce the idea of organisations responding to social expectations, then explain institutional isomorphism with practical examples from business, and finally discuss why organisations sometimes resist institutional pressure.*

The second prompt performs several important functions simultaneously. It clarifies the audience, establishes the learning objective, and structures the logical sequence of explanation. In doing so, it dramatically reduces ambiguity about what the model should produce.

This pattern appears repeatedly across research prompt design. Studies of LLMs show that performance improves when tasks are clearly specified and when models are guided through intermediate reasoning or structural expectations (Brown et al., 2020; Wei et al., 2022). While these findings often appear in technical discussions of 'prompt engineering', the underlying principle is straightforward: models respond more reliably when the intellectual structure of the task is explicit.

For academics, this insight is empowering. It suggests that effective prompting is not primarily a technical skill but a conceptual one. Scholars already organise ideas systematically. Prompting simply requires making that organisation visible.

A useful way to think about prompts is to imagine that the model is a capable research assistant who has read widely but lacks contextual awareness of your specific project. The assistant can analyse text, generate examples, and synthesise patterns, but only if the task is framed clearly.

Suppose a researcher is exploring how AI is transforming recruitment practices. A vague prompt might read as:

> *Discuss AI in recruitment.*

The response will probably mention algorithmic screening, bias concerns, and automation in hiring. Such an answer could appear in any introductory article.

A more carefully framed prompt might say:

> *I am writing a research paper on the organisational consequences of AI-driven recruitment tools. Identify three ways these tools might change managerial decision-making in hiring. For each change, explain the underlying mechanism and one possible ethical concern.*

Here, the prompt communicates the research orientation. The model is no longer asked merely to describe technology; it is asked to analyse organisational consequences. The shift seems small, yet it significantly alters the nature of the response.

By analysing relationships between words across long sequences of text, LLMs generate text (Vaswani et al., 2017). When a prompt includes clear signals about structure or reasoning steps, the model can organise its output accordingly. Without such signals, it defaults to patterns that frequently appear in its training data – typically introductory explanations or widely circulated summaries.

In other words, the model is not deciding what is most insightful. It is estimating what is statistically likely.

Effective prompts intervene in this process by steering the model toward more deliberate patterns of reasoning.

8. THE ROLE OF STRUCTURE IN PROMPTING

One of the most reliable ways to improve outputs is to introduce structure into the prompt. Structure reduces uncertainly about how the response should be organised.

This does not require complex language. In fact, simple structural cues often work best.

Imagine asking a model to help generate discussion questions for a classroom session on leadership. A lecturer might initially try:

> *Give discussion questions about ethical leadership.*

The model will likely generate generic questions that could appear in any textbook.

Adding structure transforms the request:

> *Create five discussion questions about leadership.*
>
> *Two questions should encourage students to analyse real organisational dilemmas.*
>
> *Two should invite students to reflect on personal values in leadership decisions. One should challenge the idea that ethical leadership is always effective.*

The second prompt does something subtle but powerful. It shapes the intellectual diversity of the questions. Instead of producing a repetitive list, the model must now generate prompts that address different dimensions of the topic.

Researchers studying prompting often describe this approach as task decomposition – breaking a complex request into smaller conceptual steps (Reynolds & McDonell, 2021). For academics, however, the idea is simply a familiar pedagogical technique: divide a topic into meaningful parts so that each can be explored clearly.

This principle becomes particularly valuable when working with complex reasoning tasks. LLMs can struggle with multi-step reasoning, especially when the steps are implicit. Experiments by Wei et al. (2022) demonstrated that prompting models to articulate intermediate reasoning significantly improves performance on mathematical and logical tasks. This method, known as chain-of-thought prompting, works because it encourages the model to construct the reasoning path explicitly rather than attempting to jump directly to a conclusion.

Although much of the early research on chain-of-thought prompting focused on numerical reasoning, the principle is equally useful in academic contexts.

For example, a researcher exploring corporate sustainability might ask:

> *Explain why some companies adopt sustainability initiatives primarily for reputational reasons.*

The model might provide a brief answer referencing stakeholder expectations of regulatory pressure.

But if the prompt encourages reasoning:

> *Explain why some companies adopt sustainability initiatives primarily for reputational reasons.*
>
> *First identify the stakeholder groups involved.*
>
> *Then explain how reputational pressure influences managerial decisions. Finally describe one risk of reputation-driven sustainability strategies.*

The response becomes more analytical. Each step provides scaffolding that guides the model toward deeper explanation.

This does not mean that every prompt must include explicit step-by-step instructions. Overly rigid prompts can constrain creativity. The goal is not to script the response entirely but to signal the intellectual pathway the model should follow.

A helpful analogy is the structure of an academic seminar. A seminar that begins with a clear outline – introduction, discussion, synthesis – does not limit intellectual exploration. Instead, it creates a framework within which exploration can occur productively.

Prompting works in much the same way.

9. LEARNING THROUGH ITERATION

Even carefully designed prompts rarely produce perfect outputs on the first attempt. This can frustrate new users, but it reflects the reality of scholarly work itself. Academic thinking evolves through revision, critique, and refinement.

Good prompting is iterative. After receiving an AI response, review it as you would a draft. Does it cover the points you wanted? Is the tone, right? If not, refine your prompt or ask a follow-up. For instance, if the AI's answer was too high-level, you might say, 'great now simplify the explanation and add an example'. If it went off topic, you can redirect it: 'focus only on X, not Y'. This back-and-forth is essential. In effect, you are engaging in a dialogue with AI, guiding it toward the answer you need.

Scholars encourage this approach. For example, Rath (2025) highlights the importance of structured prompting and iterative refinement in educational settings.

Prompting should be approached with the same mindset.

Imagine that a doctoral student is drafting the introduction to a research paper. They might ask a language model to produce an initial outline of the argument. The outline may be helpful but incomplete. Instead of abandoning the interaction, the student can build upon it through iterative prompts.

The next prompt might ask:

> *Which assumption in this outline requires stronger justification?*

Another might ask:

> *Identify potential criticisms a reviewer might raise about this argument.*

A third could request:

> *Suggest an empirical research design that could test the main claim.*

Through this process, the model becomes less of a writing tool and more of a thinking partner. Each prompt explores a different dimension of the intellectual problem.

This iterative approach aligns with the research showing that language models often generate better results when allowed to explore multiple reasoning paths rather than committing to a single answer (Wang et al., 2022). In practice, this means that prompting should be seen as a conversation rather than a one-time instruction.

Such conversations can be particularly valuable during the early stages of research when ideas are still forming. The model can help identify conceptual connections, surface alternative interpretations, or highlight potential weaknesses in a theoretical argument.

At the same time, scholars must remain attentive to the limitations of these systems. Language models generate plausible language, not verified knowledge. They may produce citations that appear credible but do not correspond to real publications. They may also present speculative claims with unwarranted confidence.

This phenomenon, sometimes described as 'hallucination', is widely documented in research on Gen AI (Bender et al., 2021). The responsibility for verification therefore remains firmly with the human user.

In many ways, this mirrors the process of working with a junior research assistant. The assistant may gather information, summarise articles, or suggest ideas, but the principal investigator must evaluate the accuracy of the material.

Prompting effectively requires adopting the same stance for critical supervision.

10. WHEN PROMPTING CHANGES THE WAY WE THINK

Perhaps the most interesting consequence of prompt engineering is that it gradually reshapes how academics approach intellectual problems. As scholars become more experienced with generative models, they begin to recognise that the quality of the model's response often reflects the clarity of their own thinking.

A poorly defined problem usually indicates a poorly defined question.

This realisation can be surprisingly productive. When a model produces vague or repetitive answers, the instinctive reaction might be to blame the technology. Yet the underlying issue may simply be that the task itself lacks conceptual precision.

For example, consider the difference between asking:

Explain the future of work.

And asking:

Identify three organisational practices that remote work has fundamentally changed since 2020 and explain the mechanisms behind those changes.

The second prompt is not only easier for the model to answer; it is also a better research question.

Prompting, therefore, becomes a mirror for scholarly reasoning; it exposes ambiguity, encourages clarity, and often reveals when an idea requires further conceptual development.

This is why many researchers now use language models not only for drafting text but also for interrogating their own thinking. The model can be asked to challenge assumptions, generate counterarguments or suggest alternative theoretical perspectives.

Used in this way, prompting supports intellectual; exploration rather than replacing it.

11. EVALUATING AI RESPONSES

Writing good prompts is often seen as the central skill in working with Gen AI. However, this is only half of the process. The other half involves evaluating the responses produced by the model.

LLMs are designed to generate text that is fluent, coherent, and contextually appropriate. They are not designed to guarantee truth, rigour or conceptual depth. As a result, their outputs can often create what might be described as an illusion of understanding – responses that sound convincing but may not withstand critical scrutiny.

For academics and researchers, this distinction is crucial. Scullery work is not judged by fluency alone. It is evaluated on the basis of accuracy, relevance, conceptual rigour, and evidentiary grounding. When engaging with AI-generated content, these same standards must be applied.

In this sense, interacting with AI does not reduce the need for expertise. Instead, it repositions the Role of the academic from a producer of initial text to a critical evaluator and curator of generated knowledge.

To support this evaluation process, three interrelated criteria are particularly useful: accuracy, relevance, and depth. While these may appear simple at first glance, each involves a layered form of judgement that goes beyond surface-level assessment.

11.1. Accuracy

The most immediate question when evaluating an AI response is whether the information is factually correct. However, accuracy in Academic contexts extends beyond identifying obvious errors. A response will be partially correct yet still misleading. For example, a model might correctly describe a theory but misattribute it to the wrong scholar, oversimplify its assumption, or omit important nuances.

Consider the response to the prompt:

Explain institutional isomorphism.

The model may produce a broadly corrected explanation but fail to distinguish between coercive, mimetic, and normative isomorphism, or incorrectly attribute the concept to a different author. Such errors are subtle but significant in scholarly work. This highlights the important characteristic of LLMs: they generate responses based on patterns of language, not mechanisms of verification. As a result, they produce statements that are linguistically plausible but epistemically weak (Ji et al., 2023).

For academics, evaluating accuracy therefore involves asking more than 'is this correct?' It requires questions such as:

- Are key concepts represented correctly?
- Are theoretical attributions accurate?

- Are there omissions that distort understanding?
- Does the explanation align with established literature?

In practice, this means that AI-generated content should be treated as a first draft of understanding, not a final source of truth. Verification against primary sources remains essential.

11.2. Relevance

While accuracy concerns correctness, relevance concerns alignment. A response may be factually accurate yet fail to address the specific intent of the prompt. This often occurs when problems are underspecified. For example:

Discuss leadership.

This prompt may generate a general overview of leadership theories, but the response may not align with the user's underlying need – whether that is to explore ethical leadership, compare theoretical frameworks, or analyse empirical findings.

Relevance, therefore, is not simply about whether the topic is addressed; rather, it is about whether the response engages with the intellectual purpose of the prompt.

A more precise prompt might be:

Compare transformation and transactional leadership in the context of organisational change.

Even then, evaluation is necessary. Does the response actually compare the two frameworks, or does it merely describe them separately? Does it address organisational change explicitly, or does it remain generic?

Evaluating relevance involves asking:

- Does the response directly address the question posed?
- Does it engage with the specified context or framework?
- Does it prioritise the most important aspects of the task?

If the answer to these questions is unclear, the issue often lies not only in the response but also in the design of the prompt itself. In this way, evaluating relevance becomes a feedback mechanism. It helps users refine prompts so that subsequent outputs align more closely with their intellectual objectives.

11.3. Depth

Perhaps the most subtle and most important criterion is depth. AI-generated responses often excel at producing clear and structured summaries. It requires analysis, critique, and conceptual integration.

A response may accurately describe a theory yet remain superficial if it does not engage with its implications, limitations, or underlying assumptions.

For example, consider the difference between the following responses:

- A descriptive response that outlines the key features of institutional theory.
- An analytical response that examines how institutional theory explains organisational conformity and where it may fall short.

The second demonstrates greater depth because it moves beyond description to interpretation. Encouraging depth often requires both careful prompting and critical evaluation. Users may need to explicitly request analytical engagement:

- 'Discuss the limitations of this theory.'
- 'Compare this perspective with alternated frameworks.'
- 'Provide a critical evaluation supported by examples.'

When evaluating depth, useful questions include:

- Does the response go beyond description to analysis?
- Does it engage with multiple perspectives?
- Does it demonstrate conceptual clarity and integration?
- Does it raise further questions or insights?

In many cases, depth is not achieved in a single response. It emerges through iterative interaction; their follow-up problems progressively refine and extend the discussion.

12. FLAWS ASSOCIATED WITH LLMs

Despite rapid advancement in LLMs, it has been found that responses generated by LLMs can be facially incorrect (Thorbecke, 2023). LLMs are capable of producing outcomes which are inaccurate, misleading, and sometimes completely made up. Below, we discuss the two most prominent flaws associated with LLMs.

12.1. Hallucinations

One of the most widely discussed limitations of LLMs is the phenomenon known as hallucination (Weise & Metz, 2023).

Hallucination describes underlying limitations of Gen AI systems. Hallucination refers to situations where the model generates information that appears plausible but is factually incorrect (Ji et al., 2023). For example, as discussed above, a model might generate a convincing-looking academic citation that does not actually exist. This behaviour occurs because language models are designed to produce coherent text rather than verified facts.

In contrast, criteria such as accuracy, relevance, and depth provide a framework for users to identify and assess these limitations in practice. For instance, hallucinations most visibly appear as failures of accuracy, but they may also manifest as irrelevant elaborations or superficially detailed but conceptually weak explanations. In this sense, evaluation criteria act as diagnostic tools, enabling users to critically examine AI outputs rather than accepting them at face value.

For academics, this limitation has important implications. AI-generated information should always be treated as provisional and checked against reliable sources.

Prompt design can reduce hallucination by encouraging cautious responses. For example:

> *If you are uncertain about a reference, indicate that the information may require verification.*

Or

You can also use a general-purpose fine-tuning recipe for retrieval-augmented generation (RAG) – models which combine pre-trained parametric and non-parametric memory for language generation (Lewis et al., 2020).

However, no prompt can eliminate hallucinations entirely. Human judgement remains essential.

12.2. Biases

Beyond issues of accuracy and hallucination, LLMs can also perpetuate harmful bias. These systems are trained on vast datasets drawn from the

Internet, books, and other textual sources. When this scale enables impressive fluency and versatility, it also means that LLMs inevitably absorb and reproduce the historical, cultural, and social biases embedded in the training data. Biases in AI are therefore not an accidental flaw but a structural characteristic of how these systems learn. For example, an MIT student with Asian roots asked AI to turn her photo into a professional looking headshot (Buell, 2023). The image hence generated showed her with a lighter skin tone and blue eyes. The CEO of ChatGPT, Sam Altman, also recognises that LLMs do contain biases and can produce outcomes that can be non-inclusive (Yu, 2023).

Such instances are not isolated. Research across AI systems has consistently shown patterns where outputs may:

- Associate certain professions with particular genders (Associational Bias).
- Reinforce stereotypes linked to ethnicity or nationality (Normative Bias).
- Privilege dominant cultural norms while marginalising others (Representational Bias).

These patterns highlight an important shift in how bias operates. In traditional systems, bias might arise from explicit rules and decisions made by designers. In LLMs, bias is often emergent – arising from statistical patterns in data rather than intentional design choices. Thus, bias is not a solved problem but a continuing area of technical and ethical concern.

In academic settings, the implications of bias are particularly significant. First, biased outputs can distort knowledge production. If researchers rely uncritically on AI-generated summaries or interpretations, they may inadvertently reproduce skewed perspectives or overlook marginalised viewpoints. Second, bias can affect pedagogical practices. Educators using generated content for teaching materials must ensure that examples, case studies, and narratives do not reinforce stereotypes or exclusions.

However, rather than viewing bias as a reason to reject the right systems altogether, it may be more productive to see it as a reason to engage with them more thoughtfully and critically.

13. CONCLUSION

LLMs represent a new form of intellectual technology. Like previous technologies – from the printing press to search engines – they reshape how knowledge is accessed, organised, and communicated.

However, their usefulness depends heavily on how they are used.

Prompts function as the interface between human reasoning and machine generation. When prompts are vague or poorly structured, the resulting outputs tend to be generic and superficial. When prompts are carefully designed, however, they can guide AI systems toward more meaningful contributions.

For academics and researchers, learning to craft effective prompts therefore becomes an important capability. It allows scholars to interact with AI systems not simply as tools but as partners in exploratory thinking.

In the next chapter, we build on these foundations by demonstrating how prompt engineering can support specific academic activities such as research design, literature exploration, and teaching preparations.

REFERENCES

Bender, E. M., Gebru, T., McMillan-Major, A., & Shmitchell, S. (2021). On the dangers of stochastic parrots: Can language models be too big? In *Proceedings of the ACM Conference on Fairness, Accountability, and Transparency* (pp. 610–623). Association for Computing Machinery.

Boden, M. A. (2004). *The creative mind: Myths and mechanisms* (2nd ed.). Routledge.

Brown, T. B., Mann, B., Ryder, N., Subbiah, M., Kaplan, J., Dhariwal, P., Neelakantan, A., Shyam, P., Sastry, G., Askell, A., Agarwal, S., Herbert-Voss, A., Krueger, G., Henighan, T., Child, R., Ramesh, A., Ziegler, D. M., Wu, J., Winter, C., ... Amodei, D. (2020). Language models are few-shot learners. *Advances in Neural Information Processing Systems, 33*, 1877–1901.

Budie, R., Liu F., Zhang, A., & Cionca, E. (2023). *Prompt structure in conversations with generative AI*. NN/G. Retrieved April 4, 2026, from https://www.nngroup.com/articles/ai-prompt-structure/

Buell, S. (2023, August 24). *Do AI generated images have racial blind spots? See an example*. The Boston Globe. https://www.bostonglobe.com/2023/07/19/business/an-mit-student-asked-ai-make-her-headshot-more-professional-it-gave-her-lighter-skin-blue-eyes

Cook, J. (2023, June 26). *How to write effective prompts for ChatGPT: 7 Essential steps for best results*. Forbes. https://www.forbes.com/sites/

jodiecook/2023/06/26/how-to-write-effective-prompts-for-chatgpt-7-essential-steps-for-best-results/?sh=5a76b51e2a18

Correia, AP., Hickey, S., & Xu, F. (2025). Realizing the possibilities of the large language models: Strategies for prompt engineering in educational inquiries. *Theory into Practice*, *64*(4), 434–447.

DiMaggio, J. P., & Powell, W. (1983). The iron cage revisited: Institutional isomorphism and collective rationality in organizational fields. *American Sociological Review*, *48*(2), 147–160

Ji, Z., Lee, N., Frieske, R., Yu, T., Su, D., Xu, Y., Ishii, E., Bang, Y. J., Madotto, A., & Fung, P. (2023). Survey of hallucination in natural language generation. *ACM Computing Surveys*, *55*(12), 1–38.

Johnmaeda. (2023, May 23). *Prompt engineering overview*. Microsoft Learn. https://learn.microsoft.com/en-us/semantic-kernel/prompt-engineering

Kaplan, J., McCandlish, S., Henighan, T., Brown, T. B., Chess, B., Child, R., Gray, S., Radford, A., Wu, J., & Amodei, D. (2020). Scaling laws for neural language models. *arXiv:2001.08361*. https://doi.org/10.48550/arXiv.2001.08361

Kojima, T., Gu, S., Reid, M., Matsuo, Y., & Iwasawa, Y. (2022). Large language models are zero-shot reasoners. *Advances in Neural Information Processing Systems*, *35*, 22199–22213.

Lee, D., & Palmer, E. (2025). Prompt engineering in higher education: A systematic review to help inform curricula. *International Journal of Educational Technology in Higher Education*, 22, Article 7. https://doi.org/10.1186/s41239-025-00503-7

Lewis, P., Perez, E., Piktus, A., Petroni, F., Karpukhin, V., Goyal, N., Küttler, N., Lewis, M., Yih, W., Rocktäschel, T., Riedel, S., & Kiela., D. (2020). *Retrieval-augmented generation for knowledge-intensive NLP tasks* [Conference paper]. In NIPS'20: Proceedings of the 34th international conference on neural information processing systems (pp. 9459–9947). https://doi.org/10.48550/arXiv.2005.11401

Liu, P., Yuan, W., Fu, J., Jiang, Z., Hayashi, H., & Neubig, G. (2023). Pre-train, prompt, and predict: A systematic survey of prompting methods in NLP. *ACM Computing Surveys*, *55*, 1–35.

Mercer, N., & Littleton, K. (2007). *Dialogue and the development of children's thinking*. Routledge.

Mollick, E. (2023, March 29). *How to use AI to do practical stuff: A new guide*. One Useful Thing. https://www.oneusefulthing.org/p/how-to-use-ai-to-do-practical-stuff

Rath, A. (2025). *Structured prompting and feedback-guided reasoning with LLMs for data interpretation*. https://doi.org/10.48550/arXiv.2505.01636

Reynolds, L., & McDonell, K. (2021). *Prompt programming for large language models: Beyond the few-shot paradigm*. arXiv preprint. *arXiv:2102.07350*.

Risko, E. F., & Gilbert, S. J. (2016). Cognitive offloading. *Trends in Cognitive Sciences*, *20*(9), 676–688.

Thorbecke, C. (2023, January 25). *Plagued with errors: A news outlet's decision to write stories with AI backfires*. CNN Business. https://edition.cnn.com/2023/01/25/tech/cnet-ai-tool-news-stories

Touvron, H., Lavril, T., Izacard, G., Martinet, X., Lachaux, M.-A., Lacroix, T., Rozière, B., Goyal, N., Hambro, E., Azhar, F., Rodriguez, A., Joulin, A., Grave, E., & Lample, G. (2023). LLaMA: Open and efficient foundation language models.*arXiv*. https://doi.org/10.48550/arXiv.2302.13971

Vaswani, A., Shazeer, N., Parmar, N., Uszkoreit, J., Jones, L., Gomez, A., Kaiser, Ł., & Polosukhin, I. (2017). Attention is all you need. *Advances in Neural Information Processing Systems*, *30*. https://doi.org/10.48550/arXiv.1706.03762

Wang, X., Wei, J., Schuurmans, D., Le, Q., Chi, E., Narang, S., Chowdhery, A., & Zhou, D. (2022). Self-consistency improves chain of thought reasoning in language models. *arXiv:2203.11171*. https://doi.org/10.48550/arXiv.2203.11171

Weise, K., & Metz, C. (2023, May 9). When AI chatbots hallucinate. *The New York Times*. https://www.nytimes.com/2023/05/01/business/ai-chatbots-hallucination.html

Wei, J., Wang, X., Schuurmans, D., Bosma, M., Xia, F., Chi, E., Le, Q.V., & Zhou, D. (2022). Chain-of-thought prompting elicits reasoning in large language models. *Advances in Neural Information Processing Systems*, *35*, 24824–24837.

Yu, E. (2023, June 19). *Generative AI should be more inclusive as it evolves, according to OpenAI's CEO*. ZDNET. https://www.zdnet.com/article/generative-ai-should-be-more-inclusive-as-it-evolves

Zhang, Z., Zhang, A., Li, M., & Smola, A. (2022). Automatic chain of thought prompting in large language models. *arXiv:2210.03493*. https://doi.org/10.48550/arXiv.2210.03493

3

ITERATIVE REFINEMENT AND PROMPT OPTIMISATION

ABSTRACT

Prompt engineering requires customisation to suit various academic disciplines effectively. Each field has unique terminologies, methodologies, and contextual nuances. For instance, prompts in humanities might focus on critical analysis and interpretation of texts, whereas prompts in science and technology may emphasise data analysis and experimental design. By understanding the specific needs and objectives of each discipline, prompts can be crafted to elicit relevant and in-depth responses. This tailored approach ensures that the artificial intelligence (AI)-generated content is accurate, contextually appropriate, and valuable to students, educators, and researchers within those fields. Integrating AI-powered tools into academic settings offers practical strategies for enhancing learning and research. These tools can assist in generating study guides, summarising research papers, and providing real-time feedback on academic writing. For students, AI can offer personalised learning experiences and aid in problem-solving. Educators can leverage AI to develop adaptive teaching materials and streamline administrative tasks. Researchers benefit from AI's ability to handle large datasets, automate literature reviews, and suggest innovative research directions. By adopting these AI-powered tools, the academic community can improve efficiency, foster creativity, and support a more dynamic and responsive educational environment. This chapter delves into these sub-topics, providing comprehensive insights and practical applications of iterative refinement and prompt optimisation in academia.

Keywords: Prompt engineering; iterative refinement; prompt optimisation; prompt design; prompts for academics

Chapter Goal: Explore different techniques of prompt engineering

The previous chapter outlines the fundamentals of crafting effective prompts for large language models (LLMs) like ChatGPT, Copilot, and Gemini. It presents a structured approach that emphasises clarity of purpose, audience awareness, and contextual framing, making prompt creation a deliberate practice rather than a random process. The chapter highlights the importance of aligning prompts with user expertise, distinguishing between student, technical, and research-based needs. Key strategies include using concise wording, setting explicit constraints, and providing relevant context to reduce ambiguity and improve AI responses. Various prompt types – informational, creative, instructional, and conversational – are examined, each with practical examples and their significance in education and research. Chapter 2 not only offers readers tools for designing suitable prompts but also sets the stage for advanced topics in this chapter by showing that initial prompts benefit from ongoing refinement and adaptation.

1. INTRODUCTION

The efficacy of LLMs such as ChatGPT, Copilot, and Gemini within academic environments is determined not merely by computational capabilities or the breadth of training data, but primarily by the way users interact with these systems. Central to this interaction is prompt engineering, the intentional process of designing, refining, and optimising prompts to obtain outputs that are accurate, relevant, and contextually appropriate. As AI tools become increasingly integrated into teaching, research, and administrative functions, the capacity to systematically enhance prompt quality becomes an essential competency, marking a clear distinction between casual usage and strategic, transformative implementation. In this chapter, we will touch base on four aspects to master the art of refinement and optimisation as shown in Fig. 10. These aspects are best practices for prompt engineering, ways to achieve effective prompt design, tailoring prompts across disciplines such as lecturers and

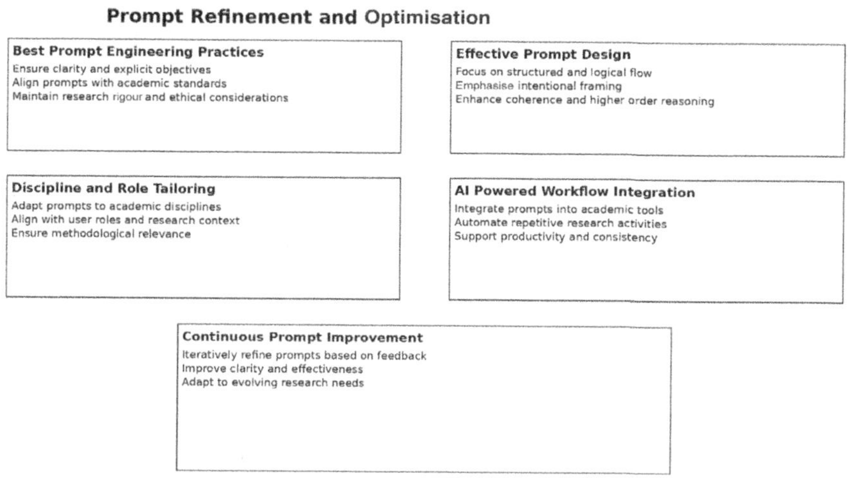

Fig. 10. Four Aspects of ***Iterative Refinement and Prompt Optimisation*****.**

researchers, and adoption of AI-powered tools to offer practical strategies for lecturers and researchers. We will introduce and study each of these aspects in detail in this chapter.

Prompt engineering is an ongoing process that entails a dynamic exchange between human intention and machine output. Initial interactions with AI systems frequently yield generic or unsuitable responses, especially when prompts lack clarity or are too broad in scope. Iterative refinement mitigates these issues by prompting users to systematically evaluate AI outputs, identify deficiencies or ambiguities, and progressively enhance prompt formulation through improved structure, specificity, and constraints. This iterative approach ensures that prompts increasingly correspond with academic objectives, disciplinary standards, and methodological precision. The chapter reframes iterative refinement and prompt optimisation as reflective scholarly practices, comparable to the revision of research questions, curriculum design, or academic manuscripts.

In scholarly contexts, the importance of prompt optimisation is heightened due to the distinct characteristics of each discipline. Each academic field features unique epistemological foundations, nomenclature, analytical approaches, and communication standards. A prompt effective in one area may yield inadequate or erroneous outcomes in another. For instance, disciplines within the humanities typically emphasise critical interpretation, argumentation, and theoretical frameworks, whereas fields in science and technology focus on empirical reasoning, data analysis, procedural rigour, and experimental methodology. If prompts are not carefully adapted to these disciplinary nuances, AI-generated outputs may lack depth, accuracy, or pedagogical relevance.

It is important to address the challenge by focusing on discipline-sensitive prompt design. Rather than prescribing universally rigid templates, it presents adaptive strategies enabling lecturers and researchers to tailor prompts to their specific academic context. By incorporating disciplinary terminology, methodological requirements, and desired outcomes into prompts, users can direct AI systems to deliver responses that are accurate and intellectually substantive. This purposeful approach ensures that AI functions as an academic assistant rather than simply a generic content generator.

Iterative refinement also plays a critical role in maintaining academic quality and integrity. AI-generated outputs are probabilistic rather than authoritative, meaning they can include inaccuracies, oversimplifications, or unintended bias. Through systematic refinement – rephrasing instructions, adding constraints, requesting justifications, or asking for comparative perspectives – academics can improve the reliability and depth of AI responses. This process encourages critical engagement with AI outputs, reinforcing scholarly judgement rather than replacing it. In this sense, prompt optimisation supports responsible AI use, aligning technological efficiency with academic standards of evidence, clarity, and ethical awareness.

Also, there is significance to positions in prompt engineering within the expanding integration of AI-powered tools in higher education and research. Applications range from generating study guides and formative assessments to summarising scholarly articles and analysing qualitative data, with AI systems presenting substantial opportunities to improve both productivity and creativity. These advantages, however, are attainable only when users possess the skills to effectively direct AI processes. Through iterative prompt refinement, educators can develop adaptive instructional materials, personalised feedback systems, and interactive learning environments tailored to a wide variety of student needs. For researchers, such techniques facilitate the refinement of research questions, organisation of literature reviews, identification of thematic trends, and exploration of innovative research avenues.

This chapter emphasises that prompt optimisation is an attainable skill, rather than a complex technical discipline. Academic professionals, including lecturers and researchers, need not possess deep knowledge of machine learning mathematics to utilise AI tools effectively. The emphasis is on pragmatic techniques aligned with established academic practices: defining objectives, refining phrasing, assessing assumptions, and evaluating results. By positioning prompt engineering as a natural extension of familiar academic abilities, this chapter facilitates greater adoption of AI technologies while encouraging deliberate and informed participation.

The chapter further underscores the importance of iterative refinement as a continuous learning process, rather than a static procedure. Academic environments are subject to change, with evolving curricula and shifting research enquiries; therefore, prompt design must adapt accordingly. A philosophy of experimentation, introspection, and ongoing enhancement is advocated throughout. By embracing this approach, academics are enabled to develop prompts that advance in complexity and efficacy in parallel with their instructional and scholarly activities.

In summary, this chapter serves as a foundational exploration of how iterative refinement and prompt optimisation can enhance the academic use of AI. By addressing best practices, effective prompt design techniques, and discipline-specific tailoring, it equips lecturers and researchers with the conceptual understanding and practical orientation needed to engage AI tools meaningfully. As AI continues to reshape the academic landscape, mastering these skills will be essential for ensuring that technology supports – not undermines – the core values of scholarship, pedagogy, and intellectual inquiry.

2. BEST PRACTICES FOR PROMPT ENGINEERING

Prompt engineering has emerged as one of the most practical and intellectually engaging skills for academics working with LLMs. Unlike traditional software tools that impose fixed commands or rigid interfaces, AI systems respond dynamically to human language, making the phrasing, structure, and intent of user instructions critically important. Best practices in prompt engineering are therefore not merely about efficiency; they reflect a deeper alignment between human reasoning and machine interpretation. For lecturers and researchers, mastering these practices enables AI to act as a meaningful collaborator – supporting inquiry, pedagogy, and scholarly communication rather than producing generic or misleading output.

Within academic contexts, the stakes of prompt design are particularly high. Teaching materials must be pedagogically sound, research outputs must be methodologically credible, and AI-assisted insights must hold up under critical scrutiny. Poorly constructed prompts can result in oversimplified interpretations, factual inaccuracies, or outputs that fail to reflect disciplinary norms. In contrast, well-designed prompts can extend academic capacity by clarifying concepts, stimulating higher-order thinking, accelerating research workflows, and enabling reflective dialogue with AI systems. This chapter outlines best practices that position prompt engineering as a disciplined, intentional, and ethically grounded academic activity rather than a trial-and-error experiment.

The discussion that follows moves beyond surface-level advice to establish a framework for consistent, high-quality prompt creation. The five subsections explore complementary best practices that, when combined, allow academics to extract maximum value from LLMs while maintaining scholarly rigour. These practices emphasise clarity of purpose, structural precision, contextual depth, iterative improvement, and critical evaluation. Taken together, they form a practical methodology that academics can adapt across teaching, research, and institutional work.

2.1. Clarity of Intent and Explicit Objective Definition

One of the foundational best practices in prompt engineering is defining a clear and explicit objective before composing any prompt. AI systems do not infer intent in the same way humans do; instead, they rely on linguistic cues to predict probable responses. When intent is ambiguous, the AI may produce content that is tangential, overly generic, or misaligned with academic expectations. Defining the precise purpose of the task – whether it is to analyse, summarise, critique, compare, or generate – ensures that the AI's output aligns with the user's scholarly goal.

In academic settings, clarity of intent also involves specifying the level of depth, complexity, and academic tone required. A prompt intended to generate undergraduate-level learning material differs significantly from one designed for doctoral research support. Explicitly stating the intended audience, academic level, and desired outcome helps narrow the AI's response space. For example, articulating that a response should 'critically evaluate competing theories with references to established scholarship' signals a very different expectation than a general informational request.

Furthermore, prompts benefit from clearly stated constraints. These may include word limits, structural requirements, or methodological boundaries. Constraints do not restrict AI creativity; rather, they focus it. In research contexts, defining whether a response should adopt a qualitative, quantitative, or conceptual lens prevents methodological drift. In teaching contexts, stating alignment with learning outcomes or assessment criteria ensures relevance. Best practice therefore dictates that prompt writers act much like researchers formulating research questions: precise, purposeful, and intentional. Let us now take a look at some examples.

Example 1: Research Context

Original Prompt (Unclear): 'Explain constructivism.'

Corrected Prompt (Clear and Explicit): 'Critically explain the theory of constructivism in education at the postgraduate level, highlighting its key principles and citing at least two major scholars in 300 words.'

Explanation: The original prompt lacks clarity about depth, academic level, and purpose, leading to a potentially vague or introductory response. The corrected prompt clearly defines the objective, audience, tone, and constraints, guiding the AI to produce academically relevant content.

Example 2: Teaching and Learning Context

Original Prompt (Unclear): 'Create questions on climate change.'

Corrected Prompt (Clear and Explicit): 'Generate five higher-order discussion questions on climate change suitable for undergraduate environmental science students, aligned with critical-thinking learning outcomes.'

Explanation: The initial prompt does not specify the learner level or the pedagogical intent, which may result in generic or unsuitable questions. The revised prompt explicitly defines the target audience and educational purpose, ensuring focused and meaningful output.

Example 3: Methodological and Structural Clarity

Original Prompt (Unclear): 'Summarize this research paper.'

Corrected Prompt (Clear and Explicit): 'Provide a structured summary of this qualitative research paper in 200 words, covering the research objective, methodology, key findings, and limitations.'

Explanation: The original version lacks structure and methodological guidance, allowing the AI to summarise inconsistently. The corrected prompt clearly states the format, word limit, and analytical lens, improving precision and academic usefulness.

2.2. Structuring Prompts for Precision and Academic Coherence

Effective prompt engineering relies heavily on well-structured instructions. Structure functions as a cognitive scaffold that guides the AI through the expected reasoning process. Rather than issuing a single, dense instruction, best practice encourages dividing prompts into logically ordered components, each addressing a specific aspect of the task. This approach mirrors academic writing conventions, where clarity emerges through organised argumentation rather than unstructured expression.

A well-structured prompt often includes several elements: task definition, contextual information, expected format, and evaluation criteria. For example, a prompt that asks for a comparative analysis may specify the dimensions of comparison, the theoretical lenses to apply, and the desired structure of the response. This layered design reduces ambiguity and enables the AI to generate responses that reflect academic coherence rather than fragmented explanation.

In teaching applications, structured prompts facilitate predictable and repeatable outcomes. Lecturers designing AI-generated learning materials can achieve consistency by embedding pedagogical structure into prompts, such as asking for learning objectives first, followed by explanatory content, examples, and reflective questions. Researchers, likewise, benefit from structured prompts when analysing texts, synthesising literature, or exploring conceptual frameworks. AI's ability to follow structured reasoning is enhanced when prompts resemble the logical sequencing found in academic discourse.

Best practice also involves using signalling language that explicitly guides the AI's reasoning. Phrases such as 'first analyse,' 'then evaluate,' or 'finally synthesise' help model the analytical flow expected in scholarly work. By structuring prompts as intellectual pathways rather than simple commands, academics transform AI interactions into processes that reflect how knowledge itself is constructed within academia. Let us understand with some examples.

Example 1: Comparative Analysis (Research Context)

Original Prompt (Unstructured): 'Compare qualitative and quantitative research.'

Corrected Prompt (Structured): 'First, define qualitative and quantitative research methods. Then compare them based on data collection techniques, analysis approaches, and typical research applications. Finally, summarise their key strengths and limitations in an academic tone.'

Explanation: The original prompt lacks structure, which may lead to a fragmented or superficial comparison. The corrected prompt uses signalling language and logical sequencing to guide the AI through a coherent, step-by-step academic analysis.

Example 2: Teaching Material Design (Lecturer Context)

Original Prompt (Unstructured): 'Explain photosynthesis for students.'

Corrected Prompt (Structured): 'Write an explanation of photosynthesis for undergraduate biology students by first stating the learning objectives, then explaining the process step-by-step, followed by a real-world example and two short reflection questions.'

Explanation: The unstructured prompt does not specify instructional flow or pedagogical elements. The revised prompt embeds a clear educational structure, enabling the AI to generate consistent and classroom-ready content.

Example 3: Literature Synthesis (Research Context)

Original Prompt (Unstructured): 'Write about AI in higher education.'

Corrected Prompt (Structured): 'First, briefly introduce the role of AI in higher education. Then synthesise key themes from recent literature, followed by a discussion of opportunities and challenges, and conclude with implications for future research.

Explanation: The original prompt is broad and may result in a disorganised narrative. The structured prompt mirrors academic writing conventions, guiding the AI to produce a logically ordered and coherent scholarly response.

2.3. Embedding Contextual and Disciplinary Specificity

Context is a defining factor in successful prompt engineering, particularly within academic disciplines. LLMs are trained on broad and diverse datasets, which means they often default to generalised explanations unless guided otherwise. Best practice therefore requires embedding sufficient contextual detail to anchor AI responses within a specific disciplinary, institutional, or methodological framework. Context acts as a filter that aligns outputs with domain-specific expectations.

Disciplinary specificity includes the use of technical terminology, theoretical references, and methodological assumptions that are familiar within a field. For instance, a prompt in sociology may reference interpretivist or positivist paradigms, while a prompt in computer science may specify algorithmic constraints or performance metrics. By embedding such cues, users signal not only what topic to address but also how that topic should be approached intellectually.

Contextual grounding is equally important in teaching scenarios. When AI is used to generate examples, scenarios, or assessments, aligning the prompt with curricular content, institutional policies, or cultural considerations improves relevance and usability. Stating the educational context – such as course level, learning outcomes, or assessment format – ensures that the AI output supports rather than disrupts instructional design.

Best practice involves striking a balance between sufficient context and unnecessary verbosity. Overloading a prompt with excessive background information can dilute its focus, while insufficient context invites generic responses. Experienced prompt engineers refine this balance through practice, ensuring that each element of context added serves a clear purpose. Ultimately, context transforms AI responses from broadly informative to academically meaningful. Let us understand with some examples.

Example 1: Disciplinary Context (Social Sciences Research)

Original Prompt (Lacks Context): 'Explain social inequality.'

Corrected Prompt (Contextualised): 'Explain social inequality from a sociological perspective using a critical theory framework, referring to class and power structures, and write for postgraduate sociology students.'

Explanation: The original prompt invites a generalised explanation that may ignore disciplinary theory. The corrected prompt embeds sociological context and theoretical orientation, guiding the AI towards an academically appropriate response.

Example 2: Methodological Context (STEM Research)

Original Prompt (Lacks Context): 'Discuss machine learning algorithms.'

Corrected Prompt (Contextualised): 'Discuss supervised and unsupervised machine learning algorithms with reference to classification accuracy and computational efficiency, targeting computer science researchers.'

Explanation: Without methodological cues, the AI may produce a broad and unspecialised description. The revised prompt anchors the response within computer science norms by specifying evaluation criteria and audience.

Example 3: Teaching and Curriculum Context (Lecturer Use)

Original Prompt (Lacks Context): 'Create an example of ethical decision-making.'

Corrected Prompt (Contextualised): 'Create a case-study example of ethical decision-making aligned with business ethics learning outcomes for undergraduate management students, suitable for classroom discussion.'

Explanation: The original prompt does not indicate educational level or instructional purpose. The corrected prompt includes curricular and pedagogical context, ensuring relevance and classroom applicability.

2.4. Iterative Testing, Refinement, and Prompt Evolution

Prompt engineering is not a static skill; it evolves through continuous interaction and refinement. One of the most important best practices is treating prompts as drafts rather than final instructions. Initial outputs should be evaluated critically, not accepted at face value. Reflection on what worked, what failed, and what could be improved informs the next iteration of the prompt, creating a feedback loop that incrementally enhances quality.

Iterative refinement involves adjusting wording, adding constraints, clarifying expectations, or removing ambiguities based on observed AI behaviour. This process mirrors academic revision practices, such as refining research instruments or revising manuscripts in response to peer feedback. Each interaction provides data that helps the user better understand how the AI interprets instructions, enabling increasingly sophisticated prompt design over time.

In research contexts, iterative prompting is particularly valuable when exploring complex or open-ended questions. Refining prompts allows researchers to probe deeper layers of analysis, test alternative perspectives, or challenge assumptions embedded in earlier outputs. In teaching contexts, iteration enables educators to customise AI-generated materials to diverse student needs, adjusting complexity or emphasis as required.

Best practice also includes documenting effective prompts and reflecting on their performance. Maintaining a personal or institutional repository of refined prompts supports consistency and reuse while fostering professional development. Over time, prompt evolution becomes a form of scholarly practice in itself – one that enhances both AI literacy and academic confidence. Let us understand with some examples.

Example 1: Research Analysis Context

Initial Prompt (Draft Version): 'Analyse the impact of AI on education.'

Refined Prompt (After Iterative Improvement): 'Critically analyse the impact of AI on higher education by first identifying key benefits, then examining challenges related to assessment and academic integrity, and finally suggesting future research directions in 300 words.'

Explanation: The initial prompt is broad and may lead to a surface-level response. Through refinement, the prompt adds structure, critical direction, and constraints, improving depth, and academic relevance.

Example 2: Teaching Material Development (Lecturer Context)

Initial Prompt (Draft Version): 'Create a lesson on digital literacy.'

Refined Prompt (After Iterative Improvement): 'Create a one-hour undergraduate lesson on digital literacy by first stating learning outcomes, then explaining core concepts with examples, and concluding with two interactive classroom activities.'

Explanation: The first attempt lacks pedagogical clarity and may result in inconsistent output. Iterative refinement clarifies instructional goals and logical sequencing, enabling the AI to produce classroom-ready material.

Example 3: Exploring Complex Ideas (Research Reflection Context)

Initial Prompt (Draft Version): 'What are the ethical issues of AI?'

Refined Prompt (After Iterative Improvement): 'Evaluate ethical issues associated with AI from a research ethics perspective by discussing bias, transparency, and accountability, and conclude by identifying unresolved ethical challenges.'

Explanation: The original prompt encourages a generic list of issues with limited analytical depth. Refinement introduces an ethical framework and evaluative direction, encouraging more sophisticated scholarly reasoning.

2.5. Critical Evaluation and Responsible Use of AI Outputs

The final best practice in prompt engineering is the critical evaluation of AI-generated output. Regardless of how well a prompt is constructed, AI responses must be treated as provisional rather than authoritative. Best practice dictates that academics evaluate outputs using the same critical standards applied to human-generated content, including accuracy, coherence, methodological soundness, and ethical implications.

This evaluative stance is particularly important in research, where unverified claims or fabricated references may appear plausible. Prompt engineers can mitigate these risks by explicitly asking AI to justify claims, identify limitations, or acknowledge uncertainty. However, ultimate responsibility for verification remains with the human user. AI should support scholarly judgement, not replace it.

In teaching contexts, critical evaluation ensures that AI-generated materials align with pedagogical values and institutional norms. Educators must assess whether content promotes critical thinking, inclusivity, and academic integrity. Prompt engineering best practice therefore includes reflective questioning: Does this output meet educational goals? Does it model appropriate scholarly reasoning? Does it require revision before use?

Responsible prompt engineering also involves ethical awareness. Prompts should be designed to minimise bias, avoid misinformation, and respect disciplinary standards. This responsibility underscores the role of the academic not merely as a user of AI, but as a curator of knowledge and values. Best practice in prompt engineering ultimately reflects a commitment to maintaining the integrity of academic work in an AI-augmented environment.

In summary, best practices for prompt engineering form the foundation for effective, ethical, and academically rigorous use of AI technologies in higher education and research. By prioritising clarity of intent, structured design, contextual specificity, iterative refinement, and critical evaluation, academics can transform AI systems into reliable intellectual partners rather than passive tools. These practices elevate prompt engineering from a technical skill to a scholarly methodology – one that aligns closely with traditional academic processes such as enquiry, revision, and evaluation. As AI becomes increasingly embedded in academic life, adopting these best practices ensures that its integration enhances, rather than diminishes, the quality and credibility of teaching and research.

3. WAYS TO ACHIEVE EFFECTIVE PROMPT DESIGN

Effective prompt design is fundamental to facilitating meaningful and productive engagement with LLMs within academic settings. Despite the increasing capabilities of AI tools, their outputs are determined by the quality and structure of the prompts they receive. In academic teaching and research, where precision, coherence, and critical insight are paramount, prompt design must evolve from casual inquiry to a deliberate and systematic approach. Achieving effective prompt design requires careful planning, reflection, and alignment with scholarly aims. Lecturers and researchers who develop strategic prompt design skills can leverage AI as a sophisticated intellectual resource, enhancing learning, research, and knowledge generation.

Effective prompt design requires an understanding that AI systems operate predictively, not intuitively. Unlike human collaborators, AI does not interpret unspoken intentions or contextual assumptions unless these are explicitly conveyed. Consequently, prompt design becomes a deliberate communicative process that necessitates clarity, logical structure, and comprehensive context. Within academic contexts, prompts should align with disciplinary standards, pedagogical objectives, and methodological criteria. This section examines three principal strategies for achieving effective prompt design: intentional framing, the strategic layering of instructions, and reflective assessment of AI-generated responses. Collectively, these methods offer a systematic framework for academics aiming to use AI tools with accuracy and assurance.

3.1. Intentional Framing and Purpose-driven Prompting

One of the most important ways to achieve effective prompt design is through intentional framing of the task. This involves clearly defining what the prompt is meant to accomplish before engaging with the AI system. In academic settings, tasks often involve higher-order thinking such as analysis, synthesis, critique, or application of theory. When prompts fail to articulate these intentions explicitly, AI outputs tend to default to descriptive or surface-level responses. Intentional framing ensures that the prompt communicates not only the topic but also the intellectual action expected from the AI.

Purpose-driven prompting requires the academic to think carefully about the desired outcome of the interaction. For lecturers, this may involve designing prompts that generate explanations aligned with specific learning outcomes, assessment criteria, or cognitive levels such as application or evaluation. For researchers, it may mean framing prompts that support theoretical exploration, methodological reflection, or comparative analysis. By explicitly stating the purpose of the task, prompt designers guide the AI towards producing content that aligns with scholarly expectations rather than general knowledge summaries.

Effective framing also involves anticipating how the AI will interpret language. Vague verbs such as 'discuss' or 'write about' often allow too much interpretive freedom, resulting in unfocused responses. Replacing these with more precise academic verbs such as 'critically evaluate,' 'compare and contrast,' or 'theoretically analyse' helps establish the intellectual direction of the response. Through intentional framing, the prompt becomes a purposeful academic instrument rather than a loosely defined request, significantly improving the relevance and usefulness of AI-generated output. Let us understand through some examples.

Example 1: Higher-order Thinking (Research Context)

Original Prompt (Poorly Framed): 'Write about social constructivism.'

Corrected Prompt (Intentionally Framed): 'Critically evaluate social constructivism as a learning theory by analysing its key assumptions and assessing its applicability in contemporary higher education.'

Explanation: The original prompt uses a vague verb that encourages a descriptive overview rather than academic engagement. The corrected prompt explicitly frames the task as critical evaluation, directing the AI towards higher-order scholarly thinking.

Example 2: Learning Outcomes Alignment (Lecturer Context)

Original Prompt (Poorly Framed): 'Explain research ethics.'

Corrected Prompt (Intentionally Framed): 'Analyse core principles of research ethics and apply them to an undergraduate case study involving human participants, aligned with ethical decision-making learning outcomes.'

Explanation: The initial prompt does not clarify the pedagogical objective or cognitive level required. The revised prompt specifies analysis and application, ensuring alignment with academic learning outcomes rather than general explanation.

Example 3: Theoretical and Methodological Framing (Research Context)

Original Prompt (Poorly Framed): 'Discuss mixed-methods research.'

Corrected Prompt (Intentionally Framed): 'Compare and contrast mixed-methods research with purely qualitative approaches by examining methodological strengths, limitations, and appropriate research contexts.'

Explanation: The original prompt leaves the intellectual direction undefined, risking an unfocused response. The corrected prompt employs precise academic verbs to frame the task as comparative analysis, guiding the AI towards methodological depth.

3.2. Layering Instructions and Structuring Cognitive Flow

Another important method for effective prompt design involves the deliberate layering of instructions to emulate logical and academic reasoning. Instead of consolidating directives into a single statement, well-constructed prompts are divided into distinct elements that systematically direct the AI through each phase of the task. This methodology parallels the development of academic arguments, which progress from introduction to analysis and ultimately synthesis. Layered prompts serve as cognitive scaffolding, enabling the AI to produce responses that are both coherent and well-organised.

Implementing layered instructions entails segmenting a task into discrete phases, each serving a specific purpose. For instance, an academic prompt might require the AI to first define a concept, then analyse its applications, and ultimately evaluate its broader implications. Such sequential directives minimise cognitive ambiguity and help avert fragmented or redundant output. Employing transitional terms like 'first,' 'then,' and 'finally' facilitates a coherent logical progression consistent with scholarly writing conventions. Consequently, the resulting output adheres more rigorously to academic discourse standards.

Within educational settings, layered prompt design contributes to consistency and pedagogical integrity. Instructors are able to integrate instructional frameworks directly into prompts by delineating elements such as learning objectives, explanatory narratives, illustrative examples, and reflective questions. This methodology guarantees that AI-generated content adheres to established educational formats. In research environments, prompt structuring enables systematic exploration of intricate concepts, facilitating the testing of hypotheses and examination of alternative viewpoints without sacrificing clarity. Consequently, layered prompt design improves both the transparency and sophistication of AI interactions, thereby fostering intellectual productivity. Let us understand with some examples.

Example 1: Conceptual Understanding (Academic Analysis)

Original Prompt (Unlayered): 'Explain Bloom's Taxonomy.'

Corrected Prompt (Layered and Structured): 'First, define Bloom's Taxonomy and its main categories. Then analyse how it supports curriculum design in higher education and finally evaluate its relevance in modern AI-supported learning environments.'

Explanation: The original prompt may lead to a simple descriptive response with limited academic depth. The corrected prompt layers instructions to guide the AI through definition, analysis, and evaluation, resulting in a coherent and scholarly output.

Example 2: Teaching Content Development (Lecturer Context)

Original Prompt (Unlayered): 'Create content on research methods.'

Corrected Prompt (Layered and Structured): 'Begin by outlining the learning objectives for an undergraduate session on research methods. Then explain qualitative and quantitative approaches with examples and finally include two reflective questions for classroom discussion.'

Explanation: The unstructured prompt lacks instructional flow and may generate inconsistent teaching material. By layering pedagogical components, the revised prompt ensures clarity, consistency, and alignment with educational formats.

Example 3: Research Synthesis (Scholarly Writing Context)

Original Prompt (Unlayered): 'Write about ethical issues in AI.'

Corrected Prompt (Layered and Structured): 'First, introduce key ethical issues in artificial intelligence. Then analyse concerns related to bias and transparency, and finally synthesise their implications for future academic research.'

Explanation: The original prompt invites a broad and potentially disorganised response. The layered version mirrors academic argumentation, guiding the AI through logical progression from introduction to synthesis.

3.3. Reflective Evaluation and Adaptive Refinement

Prompt development is most effectively accomplished through ongoing review and iterative refinement. A prompt should not be considered definitive after only one use, regardless of its initial design. Critical evaluation of AI-generated outputs is essential, focusing on accuracy, relevance, coherence, and alignment with academic standards. This process yields valuable insights into the way AI interprets directives, allowing prompt designers to make informed modifications as necessary.

Reflective evaluation means posing important questions after examining an AI's output. Did the response fulfil the prompt's intended goals? Was its depth suitable for the target audience? Were there any gaps, inaccuracies, or unclear sections? By assessing the strengths and weaknesses of the reply, academics can better grasp how minor adjustments in wording or structure shape AI behaviour. This ongoing reflective process turns prompt creation into a constantly developing skill instead of a fixed method.

Adaptive refinement may involve adding constraints, clarifying expectations, or removing unnecessary complexity. For instance, if an AI response is overly broad, the prompt may be refined to narrow the scope or specify a particular theoretical lens. If the output lacks critical depth, the prompt can be revised to include evaluative criteria or comparative dimensions. Over time, this iterative process leads to increasingly effective prompts that consistently produce high-quality academic output. Maintaining a record of refined prompts further supports reuse and professional development, turning prompt design into a sustainable scholarly practice. A few examples below.

Example 1: Depth and Scope Refinement (Research Context)

Initial Prompt (Before Reflection): 'Analyse the role of AI in academic research.'

Corrected Prompt (After Reflective Refinement): 'Critically analyse the role of AI in academic research by focusing on literature review automation and data analysis, and evaluate both benefits and limitations in 300 words.'

Explanation: The initial prompt produces a broad response lacking analytical focus. Reflective evaluation reveals the need for clearer scope and evaluative criteria, which the refined prompt addresses through added constraints and specificity.

Example 2: Clarity and Audience Alignment (Teaching Context)

Initial Prompt (Before Reflection): 'Create study material on plagiarism.'

Corrected Prompt (After Reflective Refinement): 'Create undergraduate-level study material on plagiarism by explaining key concepts, giving two academic examples, and including a short self-assessment checklist.'

Explanation: The original prompt does not clearly specify audience, depth, or structure. After reviewing the AI output, the prompt is refined to clarify expectations and ensure pedagogical alignment.

Example 3: Enhancing Critical Reasoning (Theoretical Exploration)

Initial Prompt (Before Reflection): 'Explain qualitative research.'

Corrected Prompt (After Reflective Refinement): 'Explain qualitative research methods and critically reflect on their usefulness in social science research, highlighting at least two methodological challenges.'

Explanation: The original prompt leads to a descriptive explanation with limited academic depth. Reflective assessment exposes this limitation, prompting refinement that introduces critical reflection and methodological evaluation.

To conclude, effective prompt design is a cornerstone of meaningful AI integration in academic teaching and research. By approaching prompt creation as an intentional, structured, and reflective practice, academics can significantly improve the relevance, coherence, and intellectual value of AI-generated output. Purpose-driven framing ensures that prompts align with scholarly goals, while layered instruction structures guide AI reasoning in ways that mirror academic discourse. Reflective evaluation and adaptive refinement further enhance prompt quality, transforming each interaction into an opportunity for learning and improvement. Together, these approaches enable lecturers and researchers to engage AI tools with confidence, precision, and critical awareness, ensuring that prompt design supports rather than undermines academic excellence.

4. TAILORING PROMPTS ACROSS DISCIPLINES SUCH AS LECTURERS AND RESEARCHERS

As AI tools become more integrated into academic settings, their successful deployment relies not only on technological sophistication but also on alignment with specific disciplinary standards. LLMs function based on general linguistic trends and are inherently neutral concerning academic fields. In the absence of deliberate customisation, these systems often generate responses that, while broadly informative, may lack sufficient grounding in the epistemological, methodological, and pedagogical frameworks unique to each discipline. Consequently, adapting prompts for individual disciplines is imperative for lecturers and researchers seeking to utilise AI responsibly and effectively.

Academic disciplines display fundamental differences in construction, validation, and communication of knowledge. Lecturers function within pedagogical structures informed by specified learning outcomes, assessment methods, and student cognitive development, whereas researchers pursue investigation shaped by theoretical frameworks, methodological rigour, and scholarly discourse. As a result, prompt design must be attuned to these distinct orientations. A prompt designed to generate educational materials may not be suitable and could even lead to confusion if used for research-oriented tasks, and vice versa. Effective prompt tailoring requires the integration of contextual, disciplinary, and role-specific cues to ensure AI-generated outputs are consistent with established academic standards.

This section examines how prompt design can be adapted across disciplines by recognising the distinct needs of lecturers and researchers. It explores how disciplinary norms shape prompt structure and content, how pedagogical versus research objectives influence prompt intent, and how thoughtful adaptation enables AI tools to support academic work without compromising intellectual rigour. By tailoring prompts effectively, academics can ensure that AI acts as a meaningful collaborator rather than a generic content generator.

4.1. Disciplinary Contextualisation in Academic Prompt Design

A key factor in effectively tailoring prompts across academic disciplines is the deliberate inclusion of relevant disciplinary context. Each field is characterised by its specialised terminology, conceptual models, and distinct standards of reasoning. When prompts do not incorporate these features, AI-generated responses tend to revert to generalised explanations, often missing essential theoretical or methodological distinctions. Consequently, customising prompts should commence with situating tasks within the established intellectual frameworks of the specific discipline.

For lecturers, disciplinary contextualisation is essential for producing pedagogically sound materials. In humanities and social sciences, prompts may need to emphasise interpretation, critical argumentation, and engagement with multiple perspectives. Instructions that reference theoretical lenses, primary texts, or analytical frameworks help AI generate content that aligns with disciplinary inquiry rather than factual description. In contrast, prompts for scientific or technical disciplines often benefit from explicit contextual constraints related to procedures, data, models, or empirical validation. Including such details signals how the topic should be approached academically.

For researchers, disciplinary tailoring is even more critical. Research prompts must align with methodological conventions and epistemic assumptions underpinning scholarly work. A sociologist may require outputs grounded in qualitative analysis or interpretive frameworks, while an engineer may seek algorithmic optimisation or performance analysis. Tailored prompts that specify disciplinary paradigms, research methods, or analytical criteria encourage AI systems to adopt appropriate intellectual orientations. This practice ensures that AI-generated responses are contextually relevant, theoretically informed, and academically credible.

By embedding disciplinary cues within prompts, academics transform AI interaction from a general inquiry into a domain-specific scholarly activity. This approach reduces the risk of superficial responses and enhances the applicability of AI outputs across varied academic fields. Below are some examples:

Example 1: Humanities/Social Sciences (Lecturer Context) Original Prompt (Lacks Disciplinary Context): 'Explain Marxism.'

Corrected Prompt (Disciplinary Contextualised): 'Explain Marxism as a socio-economic theory by analysing key concepts such as class struggle and historical materialism, using examples suitable for undergraduate sociology students.'

Explanation: The original prompt invites a broad overview that may ignore sociological theory and pedagogy. The corrected prompt embeds disciplinary terminology and educational context, guiding the AI towards a theoretically grounded and pedagogically appropriate response.

Example 2: STEM Discipline (Science, Technology, Engineering, and Mathematics)

Original Prompt (Lacks Disciplinary Context): 'Describe regression analysis.'

Corrected Prompt (Disciplinary Contextualised): 'Describe linear and multiple regression analysis from a statistical perspective, focusing on model assumptions, interpretation of coefficients, and real-world applications in data science.'

Explanation: Without disciplinary framing, the AI may provide a generic explanation of regression. The refined prompt situates the task within statistics and data science, signalling methodological expectations, and analytical depth.

Example 3: Research Context (Discipline-specific Methodology)

Original Prompt (Lacks Methodological Context): 'Analyse interview data.'

Corrected Prompt (Disciplinary Contextualised): 'Analyse interview data using thematic analysis within a qualitative social science framework, outlining key coding steps and interpretive strategies common in sociological research.'

Explanation: The original prompt does not indicate how the analysis should be conducted or interpreted. The corrected version specifies the qualitative methodology and disciplinary framework, ensuring an academically credible and context-appropriate response.

4.2. Differentiating Prompt Design for Lecturers and Researchers

Although lecturers and researchers often operate within the same disciplinary environments, their objectives and workflows differ significantly. Effective prompt tailoring must therefore account not only for disciplinary knowledge but also for academic roles. Lecturers primarily focus on knowledge transmission, skill development, and learner engagement, while researchers' priorities are knowledge generation, critical inquiry, and scholarly contribution. Prompt design should reflect these role-specific priorities.

For lecturers, prompts are most effective when they align with pedagogical frameworks. Teaching-oriented prompts may specify learning outcomes, cognitive levels, or instructional formats such as explanations, examples, or assessments. Tailoring prompts for lecturers involves highlighting clarity, accessibility, and alignment with curriculum goals. AI is thus guided to generate structured, educationally appropriate content rather than research-oriented analysis.

Researchers, on the other hand, require prompts that support exploration, critique, and synthesis. Research-focused prompts often benefit from explicit methodological framing, theoretical comparison, or evaluative expectations. Tailored prompts may request critique of competing theories, identification of research gaps, or synthesis of scholarly debates. Such framing encourages AI systems to produce outputs that support intellectual discovery rather than instructional simplification.

Importantly, prompt tailoring is not a matter of separating lecturing and researching into rigid categories. Many academics occupy both roles simultaneously. Effective prompt design allows flexibility by adjusting emphasis according to the task at hand. A lecturer engaging in curriculum development will frame prompts differently than when conducting scholarly research, even within the same discipline. Recognising this duality enables academics to exploit AI tools more strategically.

Example 1: Same Topic, Different Academic Roles

Original Prompt (Not Role-specific): 'Explain formative assessment.'

Corrected Prompt (Lecturer-focused): 'Explain formative assessment for undergraduate students by outlining its purpose, providing two classroom examples, and linking it to learning-outcome-based teaching.'

Corrected Prompt (Researcher-focused): 'Critically evaluate formative assessment by comparing its theoretical foundations and empirical effectiveness, highlighting key debates in recent educational research.'

Explanation: The original prompt does not distinguish between teaching and research objectives. The corrected prompts reflect role-specific priorities – pedagogical clarity for lecturers and critical theoretical evaluation for researchers.

Example 2: Pedagogy Versus Knowledge Generation

Original Prompt (Not Role-specific): 'Write about blended learning.'

Corrected Prompt (Lecturer-focused): 'Write a structured explanation of blended learning for first-year students, including learning objectives, instructional strategies, and practical classroom examples.'

Corrected Prompt (Researcher-Focused): 'Analyse blended learning as an educational model by synthesising theoretical perspectives and identifying research gaps in technology-enhanced pedagogy.'

Explanation: The original prompt risks generating unfocused content that serves neither teaching nor research effectively. The revised prompts tailor expectations to instructional delivery for lecturers and scholarly contribution for researchers.

Example 3: Role-based Methodological Framing

Original Prompt (Not Role-specific): 'Discuss qualitative research methods.'

Corrected Prompt (Lecturer-focused): 'Explain key qualitative research methods to postgraduate students by defining each method and providing simple examples suitable for teaching.'

Corrected Prompt (Researcher-focused): 'Critically compare qualitative research methods by examining their epistemological assumptions, methodological rigour, and suitability for complex social research.'

Explanation: The original prompt does not account for differences in academic workflow. Role-specific framing ensures AI outputs either support learner understanding or advance scholarly inquiry.

4.3. Balancing Standardisation and Adaptation Across Disciplines

A further challenge in tailoring prompts lies in balancing standardised approaches with discipline-specific adaptation. While certain prompt design principles apply universally, such as clarity, structure, and explicit objectives, their implementation must vary across disciplines and academic roles. Over-standardised prompts risk producing uniform outputs that fail to reflect disciplinary diversity, whereas overly customised prompts may become inefficient or inconsistent.

Lecturers often benefit from semi-standardised prompt templates that can be adapted across courses or modules. These templates may include components such as learning objectives, instructional tone, and assessment focus, allowing educators to maintain consistency while adjusting disciplinary content.

Tailoring in this context involves modifying terminology, examples, or complexity rather than redesigning prompts entirely.

Researchers may adopt modular prompt structures that allow iterative adaptation based on evolving research questions. A core prompt framework may be reused while adjusting theoretical lenses, datasets, or analytical criteria. This adaptive approach supports intellectual flexibility while preserving methodological coherence. Over time, refined prompts become part of a scholarly toolkit that enhances efficiency and analytical depth.

Balancing standardisation with adaptation requires reflective practice. Academics must continually assess whether prompts remain aligned with disciplinary expectations and evolving academic needs. By consciously calibrating prompt design, lecturers and researchers can harness AI tools in ways that respect disciplinary integrity while benefiting from technological support. A few examples below:

Example 1: Semi-standardised Teaching Prompt (Lecturer Context)

Original Prompt (Over-Standardised): 'Explain critical thinking.'

Corrected Prompt (Standardised Template with Adaptation): 'Explain critical thinking for undergraduate history students by outlining the learning objective, using historical examples, and aligning the explanation with source-analysis assessment criteria.'

Explanation: The original prompt is overly generic and fails to reflect disciplinary teaching needs. The corrected prompt retains a standard instructional structure while adapting content, examples, and assessment focus to a specific discipline.

Example 2: Modular Research Prompt (Researcher Context)

Original Prompt (Overly Customised): 'Analyse interview transcripts from my PhD study conducted in urban India using cultural hermeneutics.'

Corrected Prompt (Balanced Modular Prompt): 'Analyse interview transcripts using a qualitative interpretive framework, focusing on key themes; adapt the analysis to cultural context and theoretical lens as required by the research question.'

Explanation: The original prompt is too narrowly customised for reuse or iterative refinement. The revised prompt establishes a reusable analytical framework while allowing adaptation for context, theory, and dataset.

Example 3: Cross-disciplinary Reusable Prompt Framework

Original Prompt (Inconsistent Adaptation): 'Summarise this article.'

Corrected Prompt (Balanced Standardisation and Adaptation): 'Summarise this article by identifying the main argument, methodology, and key findings, adjusting terminology and emphasis according to disciplinary conventions.'

Explanation: The original prompt provides no guidance, leading to inconsistent outputs across disciplines. The corrected version introduces a standardised structure while explicitly permitting disciplinary adaptation.

In summary, tailoring prompts across disciplines is a foundational practice for effective and responsible AI use in academia. By embedding disciplinary context, accounting for the distinct roles of lecturers and researchers, and balancing standardisation with adaptation, academics can guide AI systems towards outputs that align with scholarly norms and pedagogical goals. Thoughtfully tailored prompts enable AI to support teaching, research, and intellectual inquiry without diluting academic rigour. As AI continues to shape academic practice, the ability to adapt prompt design across disciplinary and professional contexts will remain an essential skill for lecturers and researchers alike.

5. ADOPTION OF AI-POWERED TOOLS TO OFFER PRACTICAL STRATEGIES FOR LECTURERS AND RESEARCHERS

The integration of AI-powered tools within higher education and research settings marks a significant transformation in the approach to academic tasks. These technologies do not supplant scholarly expertise; rather, they serve as cognitive aids that enhance human abilities. For faculty and researchers, the primary benefit of AI extends beyond mere automation, encompassing its capacity to facilitate complex intellectual functions such as explanation, inquiry, synthesis, and critical reflection. When implemented thoughtfully, AI tools empower academics to allocate greater attention and resources to substantive scholarly and pedagogical pursuits by alleviating routine administrative burdens.

AI-powered tools provide lecturers with effective methods to refine teaching design, delivery, and student engagement. A significant advantage of these technologies is their capacity to facilitate the creation of instructional materials; AI can generate lecture outlines, explanatory content, visual aids, and formative assessment questions aligned with specific learning objectives. When utilised with carefully crafted prompts, such tools enable instructors to tailor content for varying student abilities, learning preferences, and curricular requirements. This adaptability promotes inclusive teaching practices while maintaining rigorous academic standards.

AI tools play an integral role in supporting lecturers with assessment and feedback tasks, which are both time-consuming and vital to effective pedagogy. By facilitating rubric interpretation, enhancing feedback formulation, and generating illustrative examples, AI enables educators to deliver prompt and well-structured responses to students. This support augments rather than replaces the lecturer's evaluative responsibilities, streamlining descriptive elements while upholding the necessity of human judgement in evaluative and ethical considerations. Such assistance is particularly beneficial in large or diverse classrooms, where maintaining consistency and clarity presents ongoing challenges.

In addition to facilitating content development, AI-powered tools enhance reflective teaching practices. Educators are able to employ AI for the analysis of course materials, identification of discrepancies between learning outcomes and assessments, and the exploration of alternative instructional methods. Through interactive engagement with AI systems, instructors can experiment with various pedagogical strategies, simulate classroom scenarios, and refine teaching approaches prior to implementation. Thus, AI serves as a reflective collaborator that supports pedagogical innovation rather than promoting standardisation.

For researchers, integrating AI-powered tools provides effective strategies for enhancing scholarly inquiry throughout the research lifecycle. In the initial phases, AI can facilitate idea generation, clarify concepts, and refine research questions. Through engaging with AI systems via thoughtfully constructed prompts, researchers are able to examine diverse theoretical perspectives, evaluate underlying assumptions, and identify emerging themes. This approach to utilising AI fosters intellectual creativity while ensuring that researchers retain full control over the academic direction.

AI tools are becoming increasingly instrumental in addressing the complexities associated with information management. Researchers frequently encounter difficulties when synthesising extensive bodies of literature spanning multiple disciplines. AI-assisted summarisation and thematic organisation facilitate the identification of patterns, conceptual connections, and gaps within existing research. When utilised judiciously, these technologies serve as analytical aids rather than definitive sources, thereby supporting scholars in engaging more thoroughly with academic materials and fostering deeper understanding, rather than merely increasing the pace of information consumption.

In research methods, AI-powered tools can help without replacing analytical judgement. Qualitative researchers might use AI for coding ideas or grouping themes, while quantitative researchers could employ it for exploring data or explaining models. Still, it's essential to keep methodological transparency and accountability in interpretation. Researchers should see AI outputs as helpful guides, not final answers, and incorporate them into their existing frameworks rather than letting them determine results.

The adoption of AI tools also reshapes academic workflows and professional development. Both lecturers and researchers benefit from developing AI literacy that encompasses not only technical usage but also critical awareness. Practical strategies include documenting effective prompts, reflecting on AI performance, and sharing best practices within academic communities. Through collective learning, institutions can foster a culture of responsible AI use that values scholarly integrity and disciplinary diversity.

For AI-powered tools to be adopted effectively, it is essential that they align with academic principles. Ethical issues – like bias, transparency, authorship, and academic integrity – should remain at the core of integrating AI in scholarly contexts. Practical approaches include weaving ethical reflection into AI usage, such as justifying outputs, verifying sources, and making clear the distinction between human expertise and AI support. By prioritising ethics, scholars reinforce trust in academic work and help ensure that AI strengthens, rather than threatens, scholarly credibility.

In conclusion, the integration of AI-powered tools provides lecturers and researchers with effective methodologies for enhancing efficiency, fostering creativity, and encouraging reflective practice. When implemented judiciously, AI facilitates pedagogical innovation, supports robust research initiatives, and contributes to ongoing academic development. The principal benefit of AI lies not solely in automation but in its capacity to augment human capabilities – enabling academics to engage more comprehensively with their core intellectual and instructional duties. As AI becomes a permanent fixture within higher education, a strategic and critically informed approach to its adoption will be vital to upholding academic standards and excellence.

6. CONCLUSION

This chapter establishes prompt engineering as a key academic skill essential for effective use of AI in teaching and research. By emphasising iterative refinement and prompt optimisation, it highlights how thoughtful prompt design enhances meaningful AI engagement, similar to academic writing or lesson planning. The importance of clarity, structure, and precise objectives in prompts is stressed, ensuring that AI responses are rigorous, pedagogically sound, and context-appropriate. Effective prompts guide AI to support higher-order thinking rather than simply generating generic content.

A major contribution is the discussion on adapting prompts for different academic roles and disciplines. By tailoring prompts to specific teaching and research goals, academics can use AI strategically while maintaining disciplinary relevance and credibility. The chapter also considers the integration of AI tools within broader academic workflows, noting their potential to improve teaching, assessment, and research productivity. It emphasises that AI should augment – not replace – academic judgement, with ethical reflection remaining central.

In summary, iterative prompt refinement enables responsible, effective AI use in academia by combining technical expertise with scholarly judgement. These practices help lecturers and researchers engage with AI confidently, creatively, and ethically as education and research evolve.

7. BUILT UP FOR NEXT CHAPTER

This chapter concludes that iterative refinement and prompt optimisation are crucial academic practices, distinguishing whether LLMs serve as superficial or meaningful scholarly tools. By stressing best prompt engineering techniques, discipline-specific adaptation, and critical assessment, the chapter frames prompt engineering as an ongoing process akin to refining research questions or improving academic writing. It also notes that AI outputs are probabilistic, requiring clear guidance and ethical oversight to meet academic standards. Importantly, lecturers and researchers need not understand technical AI details; cultivating prompt literacy extends familiar academic reasoning skills. This sets the stage for moving towards applied academic automation, integrating refined prompts into routine scholarly tasks.

Chapter 4 will apply these principles through three practical examples: automating the summarisation of academic readings, creating adaptive study plans, and organising research materials with discipline-specific prompt design. These examples demonstrate how prompt optimisation drives efficiency and scalability while maintaining scholarly judgement. By embedding refined prompts in AI systems, Chapter 4 will show how automation can reduce repetitive work yet preserve intellectual control and ethical responsibility, completing the shift from theory to practice in academic transformation.

WEB LINKS

https://www.microsoft.com/en-us/power-platform/products/power-pages

https://www.microsoft.com/en-us/microsoft-365-copilot/microsoft-copilot-studio

https://copilot.microsoft.com

https://microsoft.github.io/GPS-Prompt-Engineering-Labs/prompt-engineering

4

AUTOMATION USING PROMPT ENGINEERING

ABSTRACT

Automating time-consuming tasks through prompt engineering can significantly enhance efficiency in academic settings. Lecturers and researchers can streamline various aspects of their work by designing specific prompts effectively. For instance, prompts can be tailored to summarise lengthy readings, enabling quick comprehension of key points and saving valuable time. An effective prompt for this could be, 'Summarise the main arguments and conclusions of this academic article.' This enables artificial intelligence (AI) to distil essential information, providing clear and concise summaries. Additionally, prompts can assist in creating personalised study plans. A well-crafted prompt such as 'Create a weekly study plan for an undergraduate student majoring in biology, focusing on molecular biology, genetics, and ecology' can help structure study schedules and ensure balanced coverage of topics. This automation facilitates organised and efficient study routines tailored to individual needs. Moreover, organising research materials becomes more manageable with the right prompts. For example, 'Organise these research articles into categories based on their relevance to renewable energy sources' can help systematically sort and categorise large volumes of research, making retrieval and review more efficient. By leveraging prompt engineering, the academic community can automate repetitive and time-consuming tasks, allowing for greater focus on critical thinking and innovation. This not only boosts productivity but also fosters a more organised and effective approach to academic work.

Keywords: Microsoft 365 Power Apps for academics; summarise using AI; research using Copilot agent; digital AI assistant; intelligent search engine

Chapter Goal: Creating efficiency using prompt engineering

The preceding chapter explores iterative refinement and prompt optimisation as fundamental academic skills vital for the responsible and effective application of large language models (LLMs), including ChatGPT, Copilot, and Gemini, within educational and research contexts. It contends that the success of AI systems in academia is determined more by the intentional design, assessment, and continual improvement of prompts by users than by the systems' technical attributes. Consequently, prompt engineering is presented not merely as a single technical procedure but as a thoughtful scholarly practice closely interconnected with established processes such as curriculum development, manuscript editing, and research methodology.

This discussion has identified four interrelated facets of prompt optimisation: established strategies for prompt engineering, approaches to effective prompt design, customisation of prompts for varied academic disciplines and roles, and the practical integration of AI-enabled tools by educators and researchers. Collectively, these components establish an organised framework that elevates AI from a generic text generation tool to a sophisticated and valuable academic resource.

The chapter emphasises the critical role of disciplinary and role awareness in the effective design of prompts. Distinctions among academic fields – such as variations in epistemological foundations, analytic practices, and evidentiary standards – necessitate tailoring prompts to incorporate appropriate terminology, methodological expectations, and clearly defined pedagogical or research-oriented objectives. The chapter illustrates that prompts intended for instructional settings differ substantially from those supporting scholarly investigation, thereby ensuring that AI-generated responses remain relevant, rigorous, and contextually suitable.

Iterative refinement is presented as an essential process for enhancing the quality, reliability, and ethical application of AI-generated outputs. Through the critical evaluation of responses, the implementation of constraints, and the refinement of instructions, academics are able to sustain intellectual oversight and reduce risks such as oversimplification, bias, or inaccuracy. The chapter further underscores that, when guided by well-optimised prompts, AI-powered tools can significantly boost productivity, foster creativity, and support reflective practice throughout teaching and research activities.

In summary, Chapter 3 positions prompt optimisation as a sustainable, adaptable, and ethically sound strategy for integrating AI within academic contexts. It provides lecturers and researchers with practical methods to utilise AI technologies effectively while upholding scholarly rigour, discipline-specific standards, and core academic values.

1. INTRODUCTION

This chapter will examine the application of prompt engineering in automating routine academic tasks, with the goal of enhancing efficiency within teaching and research settings. The discussion will highlight how LLMs, when guided by well-structured prompts that articulate objectives, scope, and desired outcomes, can serve as valuable productivity tools. Automation through prompt engineering is presented as a complementary strategy that alleviates administrative and cognitive burdens, rather than supplanting academic expertise. By assigning repetitive tasks to AI systems, educators and researchers are afforded greater opportunity to focus on critical analysis, innovation, and substantive scholarly engagement.

Special attention will be given to the automation of content processing and organisational functions. The chapter will demonstrate how carefully crafted prompts empower AI tools to summarise extensive scholarly works, extract main arguments, and identify essential conclusions, thereby enabling academics to efficiently manage substantial volumes of information. Moreover, prompt engineering will facilitate the creation of personalised study plans tailored to specific disciplines, learning goals, and academic schedules. These automated solutions are designed to optimise the structure of learning and research workflows, promote effective time management, and sharpen focus. Additionally, the chapter will illustrate how AI-driven prompts assist in organising research materials, categorising literature according to thematic relevance, and improving accessibility to academic resources.

The chapter will underscore the necessity of applying automation via prompt engineering with careful consideration to uphold academic integrity and intellectual responsibility. Outputs generated by AI must undergo thorough critical review and refinement, ensuring that such automation serves to support rather than supplant scholarly judgement. When employed responsibly, prompt-driven automation can promote consistency, increase efficiency, and facilitate more systematic academic processes. Ultimately, the chapter will present automation through prompt engineering as a pragmatic and forward-thinking strategy that enhances academic productivity, all while safeguarding rigour, autonomy, and ethical standards in both teaching and research.

2. DESIGNING PROMPTS TO AUTOMATE SUMMARISING READINGS

The development of prompts to automate the summarisation of academic readings represents a significant advancement for enhancing both efficiency and comprehension within modern educational and research contexts. As the body of scholarly literature continues to proliferate across diverse disciplines, educators and researchers encounter increasing difficulties in managing, reviewing, and synthesising substantial quantities of material under constrained timeframes. Prompt engineering offers a practical solution by enabling academic professionals to instruct LLMs to systematically extract principal arguments, methodologies, findings, and conclusions from extensive texts in a structured manner. Effective prompt design moves beyond generic summaries, allowing users to define the depth, focus, and format of outputs so that they align with specific scholarly objectives and disciplinary standards. Such a targeted approach elevates summarisation from mere content reduction to an active process that enriches critical engagement with academic work.

The introduction to this section underscores that automated summarisation is not solely concerned with timesaving but fundamentally enhances the quality of academic interpretation and sense-making. By crafting precise instructions – such as requests for thematic overviews, methodological syntheses, or critical analyses – academics can direct AI tools to generate outputs that complement and support rigorous scholarly reasoning. For instructors, these capabilities aid in the efficient preparation of teaching resources, reading guides, and lecture notes that faithfully represent original materials while remaining accessible to students. For researchers, prompt-driven summarisation facilitates navigation through complex theoretical works, simultaneous review of multiple articles, and identification of thematic trends or research gaps within the literature. Crucially, constructing effective summarisation prompts requires careful consideration of academic tone, complexity, and disciplinary conventions to ensure that outputs uphold pedagogical and intellectual standards.

Additionally, this introductory discussion emphasises the necessity of critical oversight when implementing automated summarisation. AI-generated summaries are best understood as probabilistic interpretations rather than definitive scholarly products; thus, academics should regard them as preliminary analytical tools rather than final outputs. Thoughtful prompt design – including constraints, verification mechanisms, and follow-up questions – serves to maintain scholarly integrity and analytical rigour. By integrating summarisation prompts into an iterative academic workflow, automation can be positioned as a valuable extension of scholarly practice, empowering educators and researchers to engage more strategically with academic texts while preserving their essential role as critical interpreters of knowledge.

Let us understand with an example to design *Prompt to summarise readings*.

2.1. Problem Descriptions

Lecturers and researchers are increasingly challenged by the expanding volume of academic literature required for teaching preparation, assessment development, literature reviews, and ongoing scholarship. Journal articles, conference proceedings, policy reports, and book chapters accumulate at a pace that renders thorough review impractical, while manual summarisation is becoming unsustainable in terms of time investment. In practice, academics frequently require multiple forms of summaries from the same reading: concise abstract-style overviews for quick reference, structured analyses detailing research questions, methodologies, and findings, comprehensive lists of key terms and definitions for student use, and critical reflections highlighting limitations or inconsistencies. Absent a standardised process, summarisation risks inconsistency, bias towards initial impressions, and reliance on individual effort – resulting in overlooked insights, duplicated work, and diminished research productivity, particularly where collaboration necessitates unified summary formats and a shared repository for future reference.

Moreover, operational inefficiencies arise when readings are dispersed across emails, SharePoint Online directories, PDFs, learning management systems, and personal notes. Without an integrated workflow, summaries are stored in fragmented locations, lacking searchability and reusability. New researchers joining projects must often repeat literature review processes due to inaccessible, unstructured, or non-standardised prior summaries. Lecturers are further tasked with generating student-oriented materials such as simplified summaries, discussion prompts, and 'teach-back' bullet points, demanding time that could be allocated to instructional design and mentoring.

As AI tools increase in prevalence, the focus will shift from the basic capability of AI summarisation to considerations around effective, consistent, ethical prompting aligned with academic standards. Consequently, the principal challenge lies not in technological limitations, but in the absence of a robust system to facilitate prompt design, scalable summarisation, output validation, and secure knowledge base management for academic professionals.

2.2. Solution

The Reading Summariser Hub will be a Power Apps tool designed for lecturers and researchers, seamlessly integrated with Microsoft 365. As illustrated in Fig. 11, the app will feature a guided interface allowing users to upload or link readings – such as PDFs, Microsoft Word documents, excerpts, or SharePoint Online links – and select their desired summarisation goal. AI engines such as Copilot produce structured summaries based on user input. A central design concept is prompt standardisation: rather than requiring users to craft effective prompts themselves, the application will provide curated templates tailored for academic purposes. Additionally, as depicted in Fig. 11, users can choose from options like 'Structured research summary', 'Teaching summary', 'Critical appraisal', 'Key concepts & definitions', or 'Literature review extraction'. Each selection corresponds to a specific

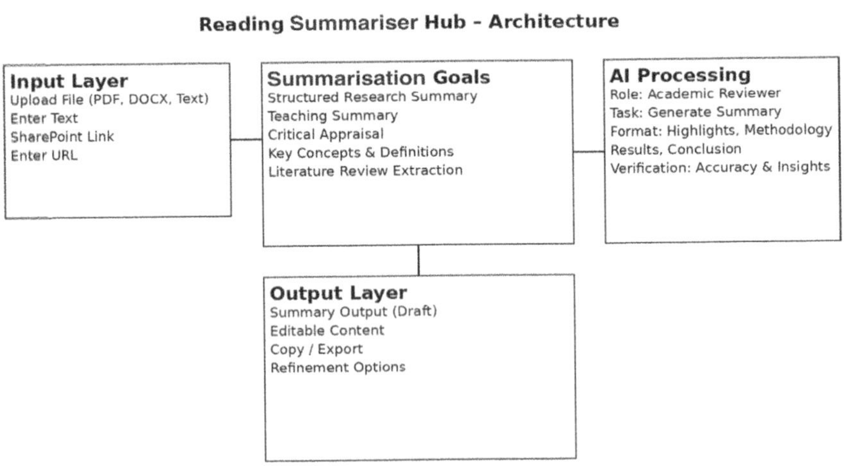

Fig. 11. Reading Summariser Hub Graphical User Interface (GUI).

prompt pattern – including role, task, formatting requirements, and verification steps – to ensure summaries are consistently formatted and immediately useful within academic workflows.

Within Microsoft Power Apps, the user experience begins on the Reading Intake screen depicted in Fig. 12. The user first selects the information source: uploading a file, pasting text, or choosing a SharePoint Online document. Metadata fields are used to record relevant details such as discipline, course or module, reading type (article, report, and chapter), audience level (undergraduate, postgraduate, and PhD), purpose (teaching, research, or both), and time budget (30 seconds, 2 minutes, or 5 minutes). These parameters will be integrated into the prompt to provide contextualisation for the generated output.

Subsequently, the user selects a summary mode, including options such as:

- '90-second brief' for rapid recall.
- 'Structured academic summary' (research question, methodology, results, and limitations).
- 'Teaching pack' (simplified summary, discussion questions, and glossary)
- 'Critical lens' (assessment of strengths, weaknesses, assumptions, and bias risks).

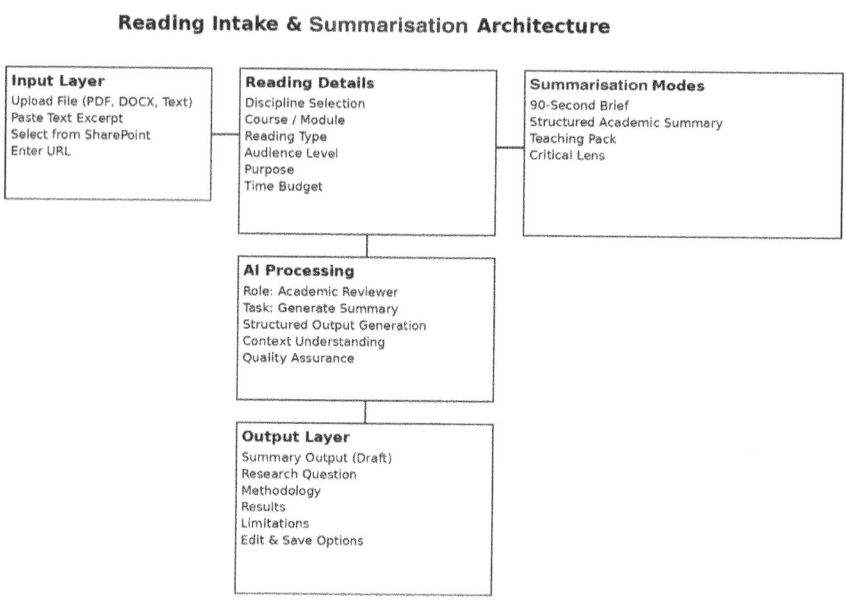

Fig. 12. End User Experience.

As illustrated in Fig. 12, Copilot will produce the output, which is then shown in an editable panel. Here, academics may refine and verify the content before saving.

The central component of the system will be the prompt composer, which automatically converts user selections into a high-quality prompt, as illustrated in Fig. 13. This prompt will be modular and will ensure adherence to prescribed output structures. For instance, the application may generate prompts containing elements such as:

- *Role*: 'You are an academic research assistant.'
- *Task*: 'Summarize the provided text.'
- *Context*: discipline, academic level, intended use (teaching/research).
- *Format*: headings including 'Core argument', 'Method', 'Key findings', 'Limitations', 'Keywords', and 'Citations mentioned in text'.
- *Quality controls*: 'If information is missing, state 'Not stated in the text' rather than guessing.'
- *Integrity controls*: 'Do not invent references; only list sources explicitly mentioned.'

As illustrated in Fig. 13, this approach aims to minimise hallucinations, enhance consistency, and promote academic caution. Additionally, users will

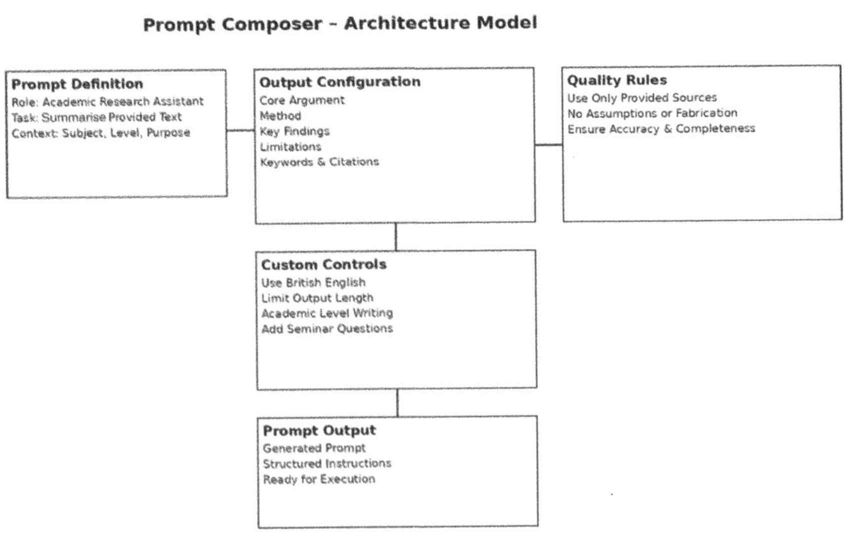

Fig. 13. Prompt Composer.

have the option to enable supplementary prompt clauses, such as 'Use British English', 'Keep to 180 words', 'Write at A2 simplified level for students', or 'Add 5 seminar questions'.

To implement Copilot within the application, the workflow utilises Power Automate as the orchestration layer. As depicted in Fig. 14, when the user selects 'Generate', Power Apps initiates a flow that (1) extracts text from the document, either through AI Builder/PDF text extraction or from stored text, (2) constructs the final prompt string, (3) submits it to Copilot or an authorised LLM connector within the environment, and (4) returns a structured response to Power Apps. The application subsequently conducts post-processing to segment the output into relevant sections and stores this information in Dataverse or SharePoint Online lists. The stored record includes the reading link, metadata tags, the utilised prompt, the generated summary, and an 'academic validation' status (Draft/Reviewed/Approved). This approach establishes a transparent and auditable summarisation trail, which is essential for maintaining integrity in academic settings.

The application will feature a comprehensive Knowledge Library and Prompt Studio, as depicted in Fig. 15. The Knowledge Library will serve as a searchable repository for all summarised readings, allowing users to filter content by discipline, topic, course, author, or relevant keywords. The Prompt Studio will enable advanced users to refine templates and generate discipline-specific prompt packs, including options such as 'Qualitative thematic lens', 'STEM paper extraction', 'Humanities critical interpretation', and 'Policy report briefing'. Over time, the organisation aims to develop a robust

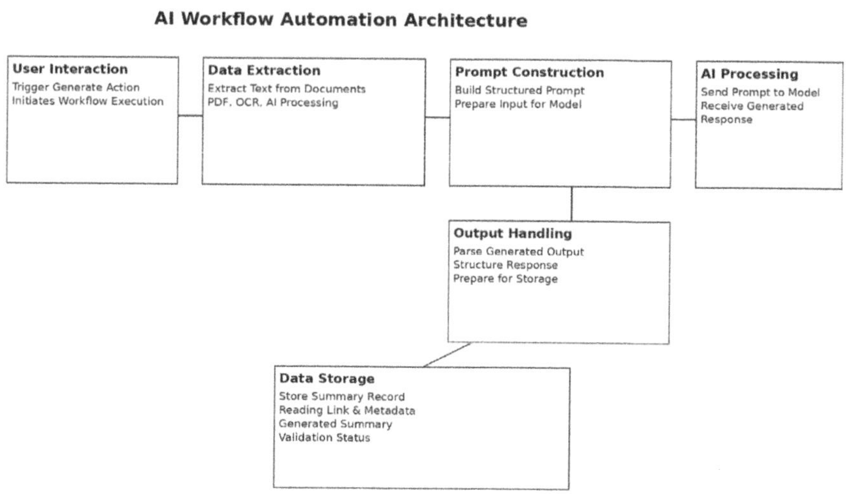

Fig. 14. Architecture Workflow of Reading Summariser Hub.

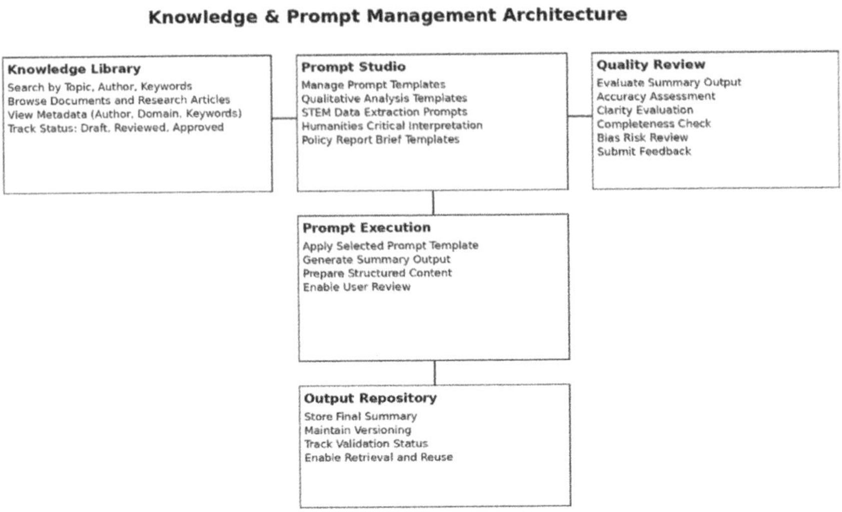

Fig. 15. Knowledge Library and Prompt Studio.

summarisation system that scales efficiently across multiple teams and reduces redundant effort. Additionally, a Quality Review screen will be incorporated, inviting users to evaluate accuracy, clarity, completeness, and bias risk – thus supporting ongoing evidence-based improvements to prompt templates.

2.3. Benefits of the Solution

In this section, we will take a deep dive into the benefits of the solutions which are covered as shown in Fig. 16:

- Efficient time management at scale.
- Standardisation and enhanced academic quality.
- Discipline-specific customisation without unnecessary complexity.
- Direct support for teaching and student preparedness.
- Enhanced research workflows and expedited synthesis.
- Governance, integrity, and traceability.
- Capability development and long-term skill enhancement.

Efficient time management at scale: The primary advantage will be efficient time management at scale. Rather than dedicating extensive hours to thoroughly review each document before determining its relevance, lecturers

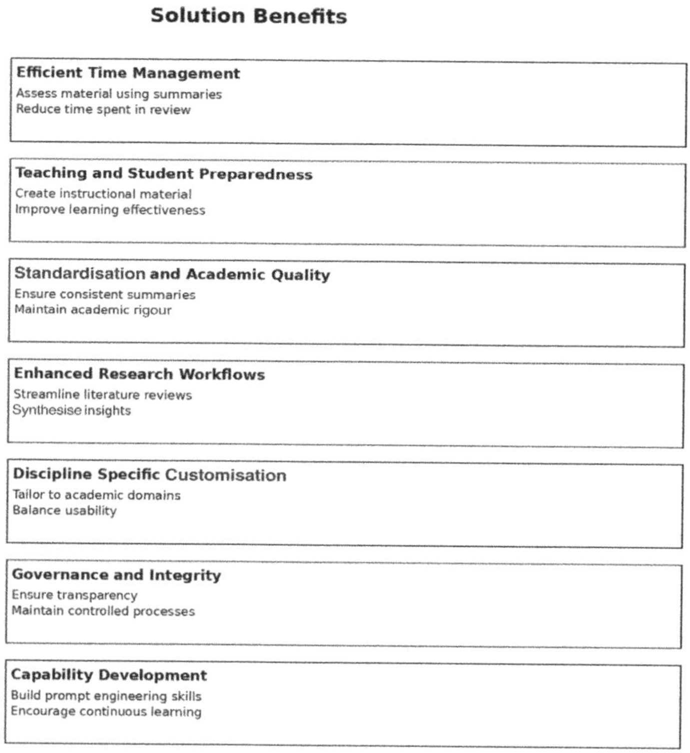

Fig. 16. Benefits of the Solution.

and researchers will utilise structured summaries generated within minutes, enabling rapid evaluation of materials as essential, supportive, or irrelevant. This functionality is particularly beneficial during literature reviews or course preparations when numerous readings compete for attention. The system transforms reading overload into a manageable process by delivering consistent first-pass summaries, minimising redundant efforts, and empowering academics to strategically allocate their time to the most impactful texts. Importantly, these time savings are not a result of bypassing critical reading; instead, the application provides a framework to prioritise and revisit key sections of original texts with greater intent.

Standardisation and enhanced academic quality: Another significant advantage is standardisation and enhanced academic quality. By incorporating structured prompt templates, the application ensures that summaries maintain uniformity in format and depth across users. This consistency reduces variability caused by individual writing approaches or incomplete notes and upholds quality standards, such as including research aims, methodological details, limitations, and implications. Summaries adhering to repeatable structures facilitate comparative analysis between papers, expedite synthesis, and promote robust scholarly reasoning. Furthermore, features such as 'do not guess' and 'state what is missing' encourage rigorous academic practice and mitigate overconfident outputs. Within teaching environments, this standardisation supports the distribution of materials that consistently align with pedagogical expectations.

Discipline-specific customisation without unnecessary complexity: The application also offers discipline-specific customisation without unnecessary complexity. Recognising that generic prompts may yield generic outcomes, the app presents tailored summarisation modes that remain user-friendly. For instance, humanities lecturers can generate summaries emphasising argumentation, interpretation, and theoretical frameworks, while STEM researchers can extract hypotheses, experimental designs, variables, results, and reproducibility factors. The inclusion of metadata, such as discipline and academic level, ensures adaptability across faculties without imposing uniform logic. This increases the likelihood of AI adoption throughout departments and enhances trust in the generated summaries.

Direct support for teaching and student preparedness: Another benefit is direct support for teaching and student preparedness. Beyond basic summarisation, the app produces outputs suitable for instructional purposes: simplified summaries, key terminology, concise quizzes, seminar discussion questions, and beginner-friendly explanations. Lecturers can efficiently create reading guides and lesson notes, which is especially advantageous for large modules with diverse learner needs. Students receive structured, accessible entry points into challenging texts, reinforcing the primacy of original sources. This fosters inclusive learning by permitting content adaptation to varying complexity levels and enables differentiated instruction and greater classroom engagement.

Enhanced research workflows and expedited synthesis: A further advantage is enhanced research workflows and expedited synthesis. The app serves as a literature review accelerator, storing summaries in a searchable repository, tagging them by topic and methodology, and enabling cross-paper comparisons. Researchers can filter readings based on methodological type, findings, population, or principal constructs, reducing fragmentation often associated with scattered documentation. Over time, the Knowledge Library functions as an institutional memory for research teams, supporting onboarding for new members and allowing supervisors to monitor evolving understanding across projects. Coupled with iterative prompt refinement, the system also facilitates deeper analysis, such as thematic synthesis, gap mapping, and argument clustering – transitioning researchers from mere reading to generating valuable insights.

Governance, integrity, and traceability: In academic contexts, governance, integrity, and traceability are paramount. Responsible AI implementation necessitates transparency regarding generated content, input data, instructions used, and related details. The app records not only the summary but also the prompt template, user selections, timestamp, and review status, establishing a defensible audit trail supporting internal quality control and ethical practices. The system encourages users to verify outputs, mark uncertainties, and refrain from treating AI-generated summaries as definitive truth. Institutions can implement policies such as labelling summaries as drafts until reviewed or requiring approval for student-facing summaries, thereby embedding integrity within workflows.

Capability development and long-term skill enhancement: Finally, the app promotes capability development and long-term skill enhancement. Continuous interaction with prompt templates, observation of AI behaviour, and prompt refinement contribute to growing institutional expertise in prompt engineering. The Prompt Studio facilitates knowledge sharing by preserving, improving, and circulating high-performing prompts among teams, easing the transition for new users. Over time, this cultivates a culture of reflective AI usage in academia, wherein prompts are treated as scholarly tools – subject to design, testing, and improvement. As AI models advance, academics remain resilient due to transferable skills in effective prompt design. Thus, the app not only streamlines summarisation but also elevates academic practices through structured inquiry, precise instruction, and critical evaluation as integral components of AI collaboration. Another example we will delve into is *Creating study plans* with Copilot as AI automation solution.

3. PROBLEM DESCRIPTIONS

Problem academic learners and educators are increasingly confronted with complexities in devising effective, individualised study plans that accommodate curricular requirements, time limitations, and varied learning needs. Students frequently encounter difficulties converting syllabi, reading lists, and assessment calendars into practical study routines, often resulting in last-minute preparation, inconsistent coverage of topics, and cognitive overload. Lecturers dedicate substantial time to advising students on study methodologies, revising schedules manually, and addressing recurring enquiries regarding pacing and academic priorities. Conventional study plans typically remain static and fail to respond to learner progress, assessment outcomes, or shifts in workload. As courses become more intricate and student populations grow more diverse, the absence of a responsive, adaptive system for study planning may hinder academic achievement and escalate stress among both students and faculty.

This challenge is further intensified by fragmentation across educational platforms. Study resources might be dispersed among learning management systems, assessment timetables within emails, personal obligations in calendar applications, and progress tracking in separate tools. Students seldom possess an integrated overview of what to study, when to study, and how to adjust their plans based on feedback or performance metrics. Even with access to AI technologies, learners may lack the skillset to craft effective prompts that yield realistic and pedagogically sound study plans. Without guided automation, AI-generated schedules may prove generic, impractical, or disconnected from intended learning objectives. The primary issue, therefore, lies not in access to AI itself but in the absence of an intelligent Copilot Agent capable of orchestrating data, applying academic reasoning, and continuously optimising study plans to promote sustainable learning rather than mere completion of immediate tasks.

3.1. Solution

The proposed solution is an AI automation system based on a Microsoft Copilot Agent, specifically developed to facilitate the creation and continuous improvement of study plans within academic environments. Integrated into the Microsoft 365 ecosystem, the Copilot Agent will serve as an intelligent assistant for study planning, accessible via Copilot chat or Microsoft Teams, as illustrated in Fig. 17. Unlike systems that address individual user queries, this agent will consistently maintain an academic perspective, tracking learner objectives, course requirements, and scheduling constraints. Its primary role will be to convert complex academic data into structured and practical study plans, employing carefully formulated prompts aligned with educational best practices.

At the outset, the Copilot figure formulates study plans by leveraging contextual academic data, as illustrated in Fig. 18. Drawing from course syllabi, assessment schedules, credit allocations, and learning outcomes, it also integrates individual constraints such as available study hours, preferred learning times, and existing commitments gleaned through guided interactions. This information is consolidated into structured prompts to direct the AI in generating balanced weekly or monthly study schedules. The resulting plans prioritise sustained knowledge development, spaced repetition, and alignment

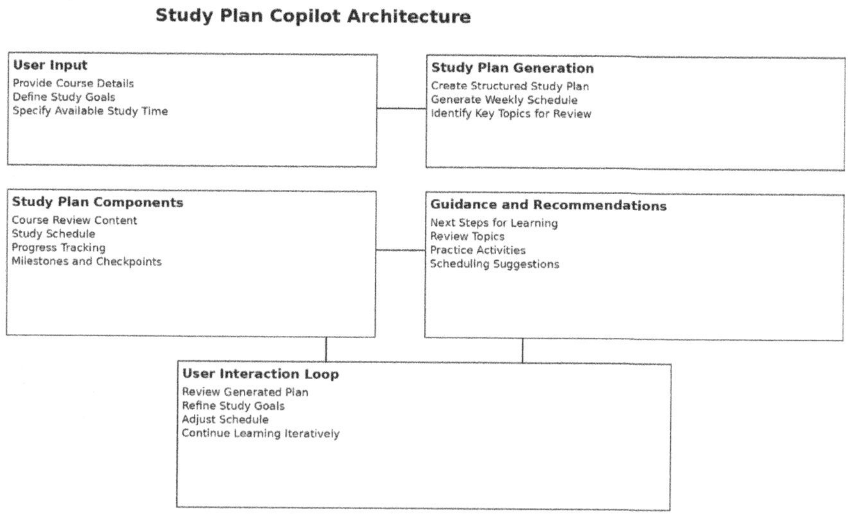

Fig. 17. Architecture of Copilot Agent Which Facilitates Creation and Continuous Improvement of Study Plans.

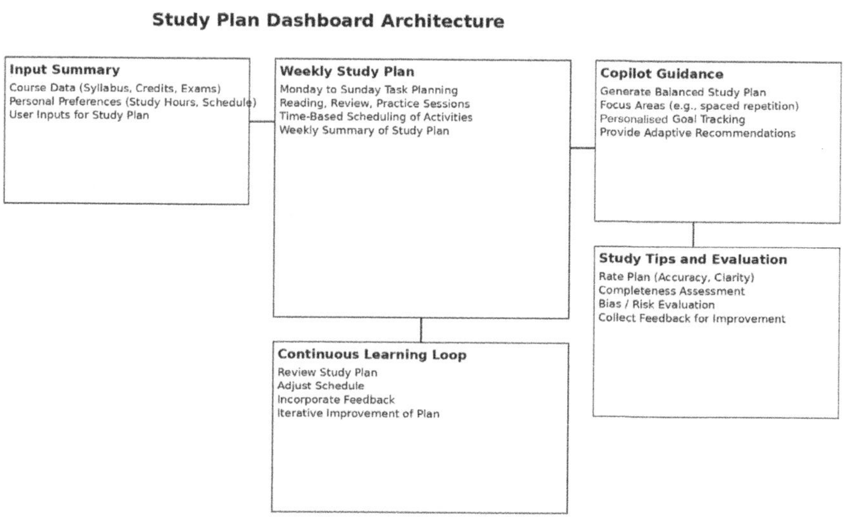

Fig. 18. Copilot Agent Generating a Study Plan.

with assessment requirements, thereby facilitating consistent engagement with course material and minimising reliance on short-term memorisation strategies.

A key aspect of the solution is adaptive refinement achieved through iterative prompt execution, as depicted in Fig. 19. The Copilot Agent will manage study plans as dynamic artefacts that develop over time, rather than as fixed

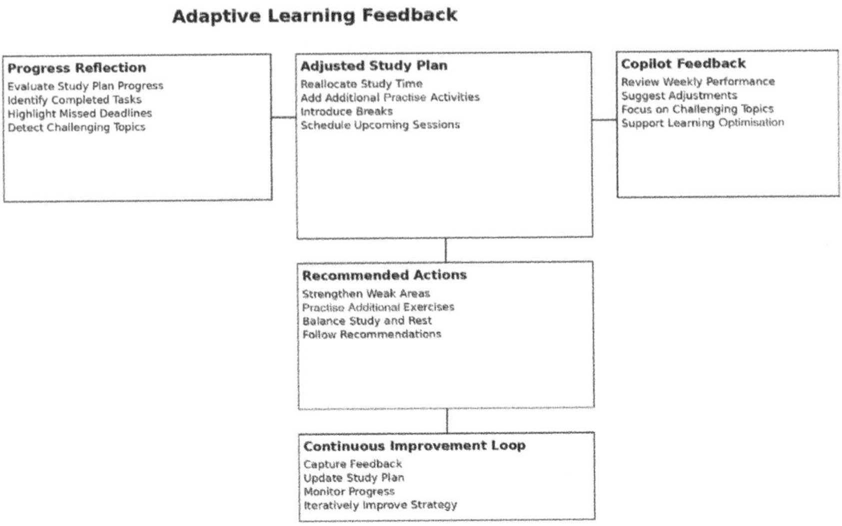

Fig. 19. Iterative Refinement of the Agent.

schedules. As learners progress through tasks, encounter challenges, or miss deadlines, the agent will initiate reflective check-ins and adjust future study allocations accordingly. This ongoing refinement relies on prompt patterns designed to foster diagnostic reasoning, such as identifying learning obstacles or reallocating effort based on performance metrics. Through constant recalibration of study plans, the agent aims to facilitate self-regulated learning and mitigate the risk of academic backlog accumulation.

The solution will adapt its functionality according to academic roles as shown in Fig. 20. For students, the Copilot Agent will deliver clear, structured plans accompanied by supportive language and motivational prompts. Lecturers and academic advisors will gain comprehensive insight into study patterns, allowing for informed guidance and timely intervention. Educators will have the ability to review AI-generated plans, recommend modifications, or approve strategies for learners identified as at risk, thereby maintaining the centrality of human academic judgement. This role-sensitive approach enables the system to facilitate independent learning while enhancing the quality of academic mentorship.

The Copilot Agent will ultimately integrate automation workflows to enable the implementation of study plans within established tools. As illustrated in Fig. 21, generated study plans will be converted into scheduled tasks, calendar entries, and reminder prompts through Power Automate. Weekly summaries and reflective reports will be produced to facilitate review and

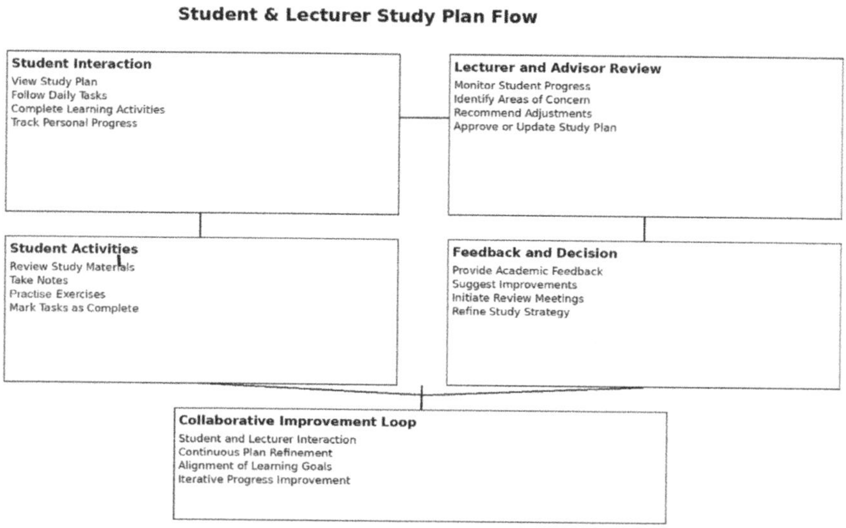

Fig. 20. Role-sensitive Copilot.

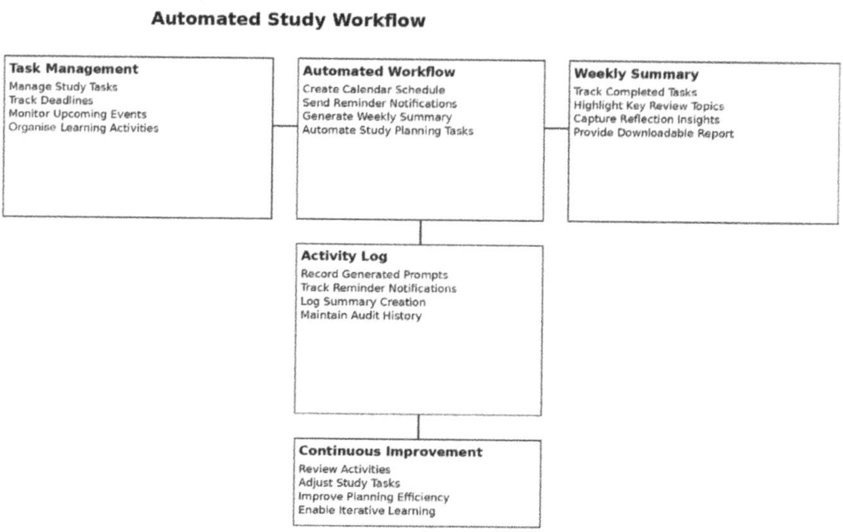

Fig. 21. Workflow-embedded Planning.

continuous improvement. All prompts and outputs will be transparently logged, allowing institutions to optimise prompt templates over time and uphold responsible AI practices. By orchestrating these functions, the solution embeds study planning seamlessly into daily academic processes, rather than handling it as an isolated activity.

3.2. Benefits

In this section, we will take a deep dive into the benefits of the solutions which are covered as shown in Fig. 21:

- Personalised study Planning.
- Enhance time management.
- Improved academic performance.
- Data informed advise.
- Ethical and responsible AI.
- Seamless integration and efficiency.

The Copilot Agent solution offers significant advantages in educational settings, beginning with scalable personalised study planning. Each learner will receive a tailored study plan based on their academic programme, learning pace, and personal circumstances, without increasing the workload for lecturers or advisors. This level of personalisation is driven by structured academic data, ensuring equitable outcomes while acknowledging individual differences. Consequently, students gain greater clarity and ownership over their learning, which promotes increased engagement and consistency.

Further, the platform improves time management and mitigates cognitive overload for learners. By breaking down complex academic goals into

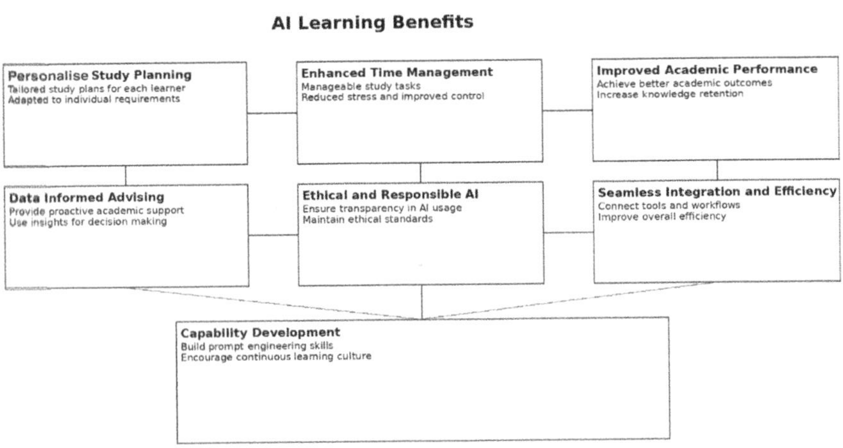

Fig. 22. Scalable Academic Benefits.

manageable units and distributing them effectively across available time, the Copilot Agent reduces anxiety associated with unstructured workloads. The establishment of clear daily and weekly priorities helps students focus on essential tasks, while adaptive scheduling prevents overly ambitious planning. This method supports sustainable study habits and alleviates burnout, particularly during periods of intensive assessment.

Academic performance and retention are also enhanced through this system. Study plans are aligned with learning outcomes and assessment requirements, ensuring proportionate effort across topics. Early identification of learning gaps and timely redistribution of study time decrease instances of last-minute failure and improve comprehension. Over time, students develop stronger self-regulation skills, resulting in improved academic results and reduced attrition.

Additionally, lecturers and academic advisors benefit from increased effectiveness. The Copilot Agent provides insight into student engagement with their study plans, facilitating data-informed advising rather than reactive troubleshooting. Advisors can detect common challenges within cohorts, customise support strategies, and intervene early when students require assistance. This approach elevates the quality of academic support without adding administrative overhead.

The solution also fosters ethical and responsible AI use in education. By incorporating pedagogical principles, transparency, and human oversight, it ensures that AI enhances rather than replaces critical thinking. Students are encouraged to reflect on their progress, while educators retain ultimate authority over academic decision-making, thus building trust in AI-assisted practices.

Workflow integration and operational efficiency are markedly improved. By linking study planning with calendars, task managers, and learning platforms, the Copilot Agent minimises fragmentation and reduces manual coordination. Students benefit from a unified interface, while institutions achieve scalable automation that aligns with existing infrastructure.

Finally, the Copilot Agent supports long-term capability development for both learners and educators. Students acquire essential skills in planning, reflection, and self-directed learning, and academics become more proficient with AI-enabled workflows. As curricula and AI technologies evolve, the adaptable prompt-driven approach ensures that study planning transitions from a reactive to a strategic academic practice.

Now let's look at the last and final solution on *Organising research materials*.

4. PROBLEM DESCRIPTION

Managing research materials in today's academic and research settings has grown increasingly complex and time-consuming. Researchers and lecturers deal with vast amounts of diverse content, such as journal articles, conference papers, datasets, policy documents, interview transcripts, field notes, and multimedia files. These resources are scattered across various locations, including email attachments, personal drives, cloud storage, learning management systems, and shared team workspaces. As research progresses, materials accumulate without standard naming practices, metadata, or classification protocols. This disorganisation causes repeated work, difficulty finding crucial documents, and limited understanding of how knowledge is structured throughout a project or institution. Researchers often waste valuable time searching for information instead of analysing it, while new team members struggle to grasp the research landscape.

Traditional document management solutions add to this challenge. Although platforms like SharePoint Online offer strong storage and collaboration features, they depend largely on manual categorisation and user diligence. Without smart assistance, researchers are left to decide how to tag, organise, and connect documents, which frequently leads to inconsistent and incomplete organisation. Generative AI tools can summarise or interpret documents, but these capabilities are rarely integrated into structured knowledge management processes. This means AI insights tend to be temporary rather than forming part of an enduring institutional knowledge base. The fundamental issue isn't a shortage of digital storage or AI technology but rather the lack of an intelligent Copilot Agent that continually helps researchers organise materials, extract insights, and structure knowledge within SharePoint Online to foster long-term scholarly research, collaboration, and uphold academic integrity.

4.1. Solution

The proposed solution will be a Copilot-powered AI agent integrated with SharePoint Online, designed specifically to automate and enhance the organisation of research materials as shown in Fig. 23. This Copilot Agent will operate as an intelligent research assistant embedded within Microsoft 365, accessible through SharePoint Online, Microsoft Teams, and Copilot chat. Rather than functioning as a one-time query tool, the agent will maintain contextual awareness of research projects, themes, and disciplinary norms. Its primary role will be to guide the ingestion, classification, enrichment, and

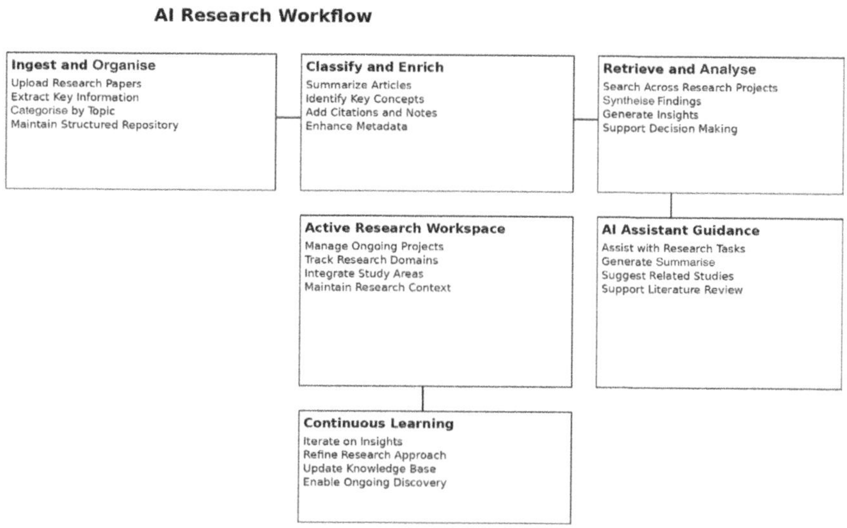

Fig. 23. Intelligent Research Orchestration.

retrieval of research materials using prompt-driven automation aligned with academic workflows.

At the point of content ingestion, the Copilot Agent will assist researchers in organising materials as they are uploaded to SharePoint Online. When a document is added, the agent will analyse its content and context using structured prompts to identify key attributes such as topic, methodology, discipline, research phase, and relevance, as shown in Fig. 24. Based on this analysis, it will suggest appropriate metadata, content types, and document libraries. Researchers will retain full control, reviewing and approving classifications before they are finalised. This human-in-the-loop approach will ensure that AI recommendations enhance consistency without undermining scholarly judgement. Over time, this process will create a structured and semantically rich SharePoint Online repository that reflects the intellectual organisation of the research rather than arbitrary folder hierarchies.

A central feature of the solution will be AI-assisted knowledge enrichment through Copilot-generated summaries, keywords, and conceptual tags. Using carefully engineered prompts, the Copilot Agent will generate structured summaries highlighting research objectives, theoretical frameworks, methods, findings, and limitations as shown in Fig. 25. These summaries will be stored as metadata or linked knowledge pages within SharePoint Online, enabling rapid understanding without replacing engagement with original sources. By embedding these AI-generated insights directly into the repository, the

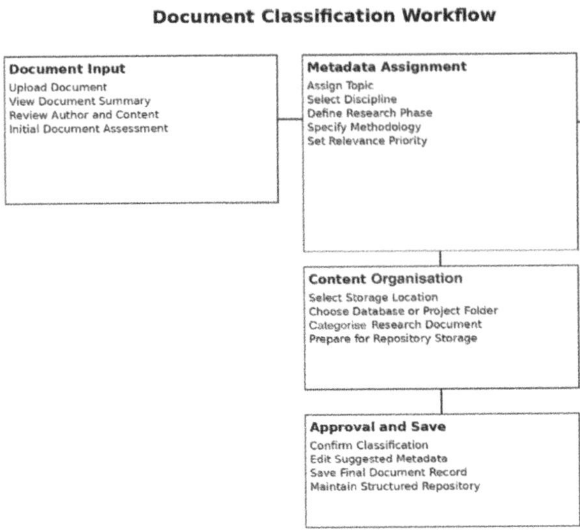

Fig. 24. Human-guided Classification.

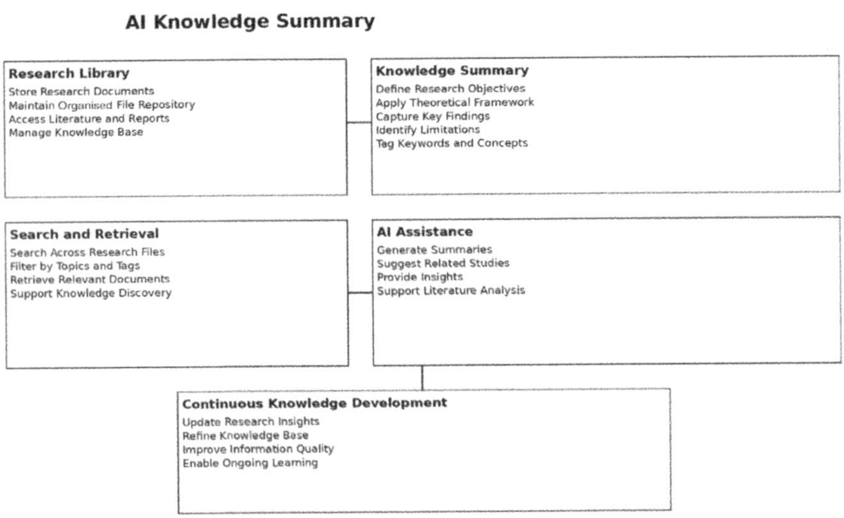

Fig. 25. Knowledge Enrichment Hub.

system will transform SharePoint Online from a passive storage platform into an active research knowledge base that supports synthesis and discovery.

The Copilot Agent will also support cross-document organisation and thematic linking. Rather than treating documents as isolated artefacts, the agent will identify conceptual relationships across materials using prompt-driven analysis. It will suggest thematic collections, literature clusters, and research strands based on shared concepts, methodologies, or findings as shown in Fig. 26.

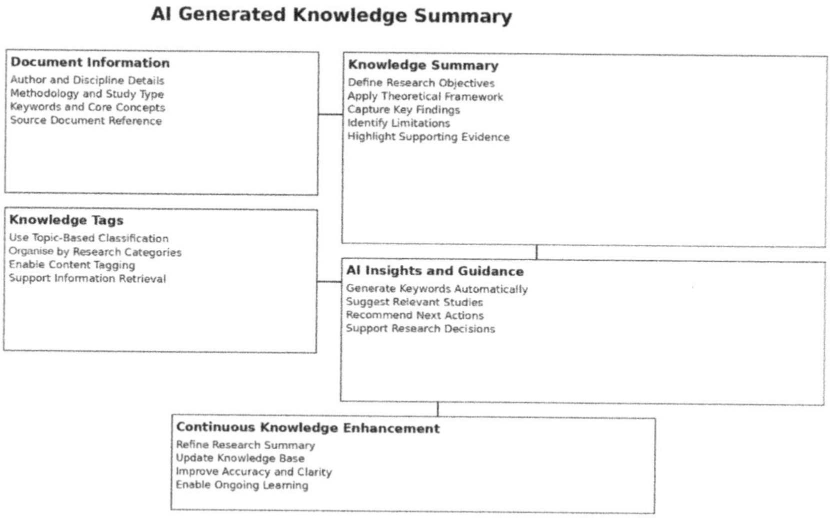

Fig. 26. AI Knowledge Enrichment.

These relationships will be represented through SharePoint Online hubs, managed metadata, and knowledge pages, allowing researchers to navigate their materials conceptually rather than sequentially. This approach will be particularly valuable in longitudinal and interdisciplinary research projects, where intellectual connections often evolve over time.

Finally, the solution will integrate automation workflows to operationalise organised knowledge. Using Power Automate, the Copilot Agent will trigger processes such as automatic tagging, version tracking, review reminders, and research lifecycle transitions, as shown in Fig. 27. It will generate periodic summaries of newly added materials and highlight emerging themes or gaps. All AI interactions, prompts, and outputs will be logged transparently, enabling continuous refinement of prompt strategies and ensuring responsible AI use. Through this orchestration, the Copilot Agent will embed intelligent organisation directly into everyday research practice rather than treating it as an afterthought.

4.2. Benefits

In this section, we will take a deep dive into the benefits of the solutions which are covered as shown in Fig. 28:

- Faster research access.
- Consistent organisation.

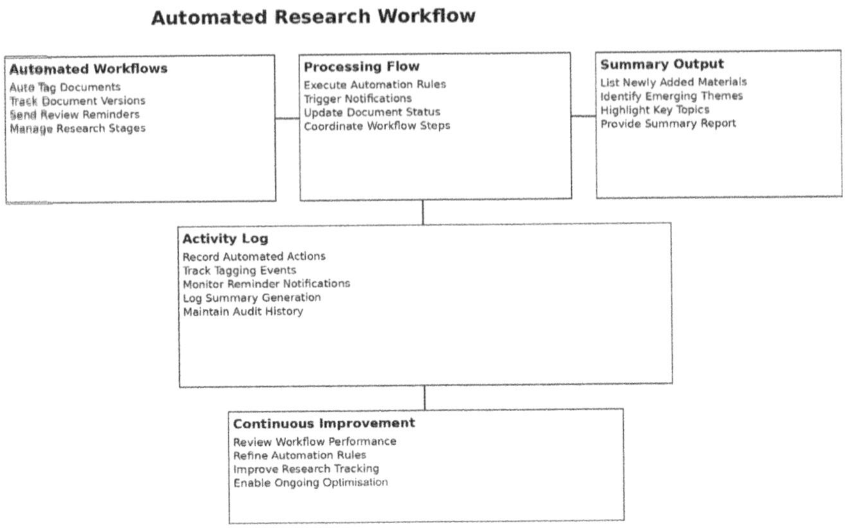

Fig. 27. Operationalised Research Knowledge.

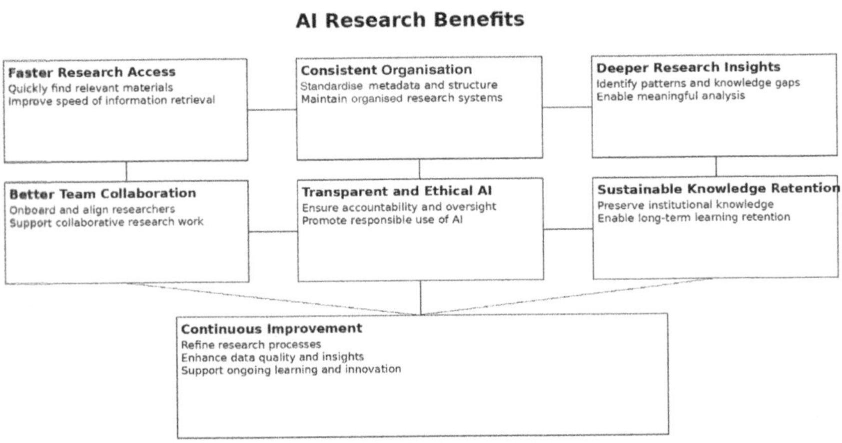

Fig. 28. Strategic Research Benefits.

- Deeper research insights.
- Better team collaboration.
- Transparent and ethical AI.
- Sustainable knowledge retention.

The primary advantage of this solution is a substantial reduction in the time spent locating and managing research materials. By organising content at the point of ingestion and augmenting it with structured metadata and comprehensive summaries, researchers will efficiently access pertinent documents. This improvement allows academics to focus their efforts on analysis, interpretation, and knowledge creation, rather than administrative tasks.

A secondary benefit includes enhanced consistency and quality in research organisation for both individuals and teams. The Copilot Agent encourages standardised classification practices while accommodating disciplinary nuances, mitigating fragmentation caused by personal filing routines. Uniform metadata, summaries, and thematic structures foster repositories that are easier to comprehend, share, and maintain, particularly for collaborative and long-term projects.

Another notable benefit is improved research synthesis and insight generation. By highlighting conceptual relationships and thematic groupings, the solution enables researchers to discern patterns, contradictions, and gaps in the literature. This capability supports more profound engagement with research materials and facilitates advanced scholarly activities such as theory development, comparative analysis, and interdisciplinary research.

Additionally, onboarding and collaboration within research teams are strengthened. New researchers, doctoral candidates, and collaborators gain immediate access to a well-organised repository reflecting the intellectual framework of the project. AI-generated summaries and thematic navigation streamline the acclimation process and promote collective understanding, enhancing effective teamwork from the outset.

The responsible and transparent utilisation of AI in research knowledge management is another significant benefit. The system incorporates human oversight, prompt transparency, and ethical parameters, ensuring AI serves to complement, not replace, scholarly judgement. Researchers maintain accountability for interpretation and validation, thereby upholding academic integrity alongside automation.

Integration with existing academic workflows and infrastructure is seamless. Building on SharePoint Online and Microsoft 365, the solution minimises disruption to established processes. Researchers engage with AI-enhanced organisation through familiar tools, increasing adoption rates and ensuring sustainability without necessitating parallel systems.

Finally, the solution contributes to long-term institutional knowledge preservation and capability development. With Copilot-enriched SharePoint Online repositories, institutions create dynamic knowledge assets that retain value beyond individual initiatives. Researchers and organisations cultivate prompt literacy and AI-assisted organisational competencies, which remain applicable as technologies advance. Ultimately, this solution elevates research material organisation from a clerical function to a strategic scholarly activity that underpins rigour, collaboration, and innovation.

5. CONCLUSION

This chapter has established that effective integration of AI intelligence into academic practice is best accomplished through purposefully designed AI-enabled systems that align with established scholarly workflows, rather than relying on isolated tools or ad hoc experimentation. Through the examination of three specific use cases – automated summarisation of readings, AI-assisted creation of study plans, and intelligent organisation of research materials – the chapter demonstrates how Copilot-driven automation can enhance core academic activities while upholding human judgement, disciplinary standards, and ethical responsibility. Rather than proposing AI as a substitute for academic labour, these examples exemplify a move towards augmentation, whereby AI operates as a structured assistant to alleviate cognitive and administrative demands, thereby allowing academics and students to prioritise higher-order thinking, critical interpretation, and innovation. Collectively, these examples reinforce the central argument that the value of AI in academia resides not solely in its generative abilities but in the deliberate orchestration of prompts, workflows, and governance structures.

The initial example involves designing prompts within a Power Apps application integrated with Copilot to automate the summarisation of academic readings. This approach addresses the persistent challenge of information overload in academia by transforming the summarisation process into a structured, academically valuable artefact, leveraging prompt engineering within a guided application experience. The solution highlights that meaningful summarisation requires clear objectives, an understanding of disciplinary context, and explicit constraints to ensure accuracy and relevance. Furthermore, AI-generated summaries gain significant worth when reviewed, refined, and stored within institutional knowledge systems, enhancing comprehension, expediting literature review, and supporting instructional preparation, while maintaining the importance of original sources and critical reading.

The second example explores the application of a Copilot Agent to automate the development and refinement of study plans. By integrating contextual academic data, individual constraints, and pedagogical principles into prompt-driven workflows, the Copilot Agent supports both learners and educators in translating complex requirements into adaptive study schedules. This example emphasises the significance of reflective and iterative study planning, where progress, difficulty, and feedback inform continuous adjustments. Importantly, AI's involvement fosters self-regulated learning rather than dependence, positioning the Copilot Agent as a supportive coach that encourages reflection, prioritisation, and accountability. This contributes to improved educational outcomes while preserving learner agency and academic integrity.

The third example focuses on organising research materials using Copilot in conjunction with SharePoint Online, addressing the long-term stewardship of academic knowledge. This solution demonstrates how AI transforms SharePoint Online from a passive repository to an active research knowledge base through intelligent classification, metadata enrichment, thematic linking, and lifecycle management. Embedding Copilot throughout content ingestion and research workflows establishes organisation as a continual scholarly pursuit, as opposed to a retrospective administrative activity. Prompt-driven analysis facilitates the generation of summaries, keywords, and conceptual links, enabling researchers to navigate content semantically and support deeper collaboration, synthesis, and project continuity. This example affirms that AI's principal contribution to research is in structuring knowledge to promote interpretation, connection, and discovery.

Together, these three cases present a unified perspective for AI-enabled academia anchored in prompt engineering, automation, and responsible design. They demonstrate that successful AI adoption extends beyond access to advanced models; it necessitates intentional system design that integrates AI into academic processes, respects disciplinary variation, and ensures transparency with human oversight. Whether advancing reading comprehension, learning strategies, or research organisation, Copilot-based solutions are most effective when aligned with academic values. As AI continues to influence educational and research contexts, the approaches described herein provide a sustainable framework for integration, enhancing productivity and creativity without compromising academic standards. In conclusion, this chapter posits that well-designed and governed AI can serve as a reliable partner in academic endeavours, reinforcing teaching, learning, and research while preserving the centrality of human intellect and judgement.

6. BUILT UP FOR THE NEXT CHAPTER

The upcoming chapter will move from organising and managing academic tasks to the application of prompt engineering within authentic assessment and examination contexts. Whereas this chapter demonstrates how AI-driven systems facilitate summarisation of readings, development of adaptive study plans, and systematic organisation of research materials, Chapter 5 will focus on converting these outputs into academically valuable assessment content. This progression will exemplify a comprehensive academic workflow in which AI automation enhances efficiency while preserving pedagogical integrity and intellectual depth.

The chapter will highlight practical academic scenarios where prompt engineering contributes to assessment design and preparation. Lecturers and researchers will be guided on crafting prompts and using of LLMs to generate effective outcomes.

This approach reinforces the notion that AI is most effective as a collaborative partner promoting critical analysis and refinement, rather than replacing academic expertise.

WEB LINKS

https://www.microsoft.com/en-us/power-platform/products/power-pages

https://www.microsoft.com/en-us/microsoft-365-copilot/microsoft-copilot-studio

https://copilot.microsoft.com

https://microsoft.github.io/GPS-Prompt-Engineering-Labs/prompt-engineering

5

PROMPT ENGINEERING FOR ACADEMICS: REAL-WORLD APPLICATION

ABSTRACT

This chapter examines how prompt engineering can be meaningfully integrated into core academic practices, including research design, literature review, assessment, and lecture preparation. Rather than presenting artificial intelligence (AI) as a tool for automation, the chapter frames it as a mechanism for augmenting intellectual processes such as idea generation, synthesis, critique, and pedagogical design. Through detailed examples, it demonstrates how carefully constructed prompts can support the formulation of research questions, the structuring of literature reviews, and the development of aligned and authentic assessments. A key contribution of the chapter lies in shifting the focus from output generation to process enhancement – highlighting how iterative prompting enables exploration, refinement, and critical engagement. At the same time, the chapter addresses important risks, including over-reliance on AI-generated content and lack of originality. It emphasises the continued centrality of academic judgement in evaluating, contextualising, and validating AI output.

Keywords: Academic practice; literature review; assessment design; research questions; generative AI; critical thinking

Chapter Goal: Prep work for research, assessment design, and exams using prompt engineering.

1. INTRODUCTION

Up to this point, we have explored how prompts shape the responses generated by large language models (LLMs). We have seen that the difference between a vague prompt and a carefully designed one can significantly influence the quality, structure, and usefulness of the output (Brown et al., 2020). Yet understanding prompt structure alone does not fully answer a more practical question that many academics ask: *what does prompting actually look like in scholarly work?*

For many lecturers and researchers encountering generative AI (Gen AI)/LLMs for the first time, prompting appears to be little more than asking questions. But experienced users quickly realise that prompting functions less as casual questioning and more as a form of structured intellectual dialogue. The model does not simply provide information; rather, it responds to the way the user frames a problem, specifies context, and guides the direction of the conversation. When prompts are treated as mere instructions, the resulting outputs tend to be superficial and generic. When they are treated as extensions of scholarly thinking, they become tools for exploration, critique, and refinement (Kasneci et al., 2023).

In academic environments, this means prompting can serve as a thinking partner rather than an answer generator (Zawacki-Richter et al., 2019). Used carefully, LLM prompts can help scholars clarify unfamiliar ideas, test emerging arguments, explore alternative perspectives, or generate teaching materials that stimulate classroom discussion. What distinguishes effective academic prompting from everyday use, however, is the intentionality behind the interaction. Scholars are not merely looking for quick answers; they are attempting to deepen understanding, refine concepts, and develop ideas. Brown et al. (2020) challenge us to reconsider how these processes unfold.

In this section, we therefore shift our focus from prompt design to prompt use. Specifically, we examine how prompting can support three common activities in academic life: exploring unfamiliar knowledge domains, preparing teaching materials, and developing research ideas. These examples are not presented as rigid templates but as illustrations of how prompting can be integrated into scholarly workflows.

2. REFRAMING ACADEMIC WORK IN THE AGE OF GEN AI

There is a quiet but profound shift underway in academic work. For decades, the core intellectual labour of lecturers and researchers has revolved around designing questions, structuring knowledge, and evaluating understanding. Whether preparing a lecture, framing a research study, or constructing an examination, academics have operated as designers of thinking – crafting intellectual experiences that shape how others learn and engage with ideas.

Gen AI does not replace this role. If anything, it makes it more visible.

What changes, however, is the medium through which this design occurs. Prompt engineering introduces a new layer between intention and output. Instead of directly writing a question, an explanation, or a case, the academic now designs a prompt that produces it. While this may appear to be a minor procedural shift, it carries significant implications. It requires a more explicit articulation of what was previously tacit: expectations about depth, structure, and purpose.

This shift reflects what Amershi et al. (2019) describe as the need for intentional interaction design in human–AI systems. Users must specify not only what they want, but how they want the system to respond. In an academic context, this means making explicit:

- What kind of output do they want for the intended audience?
- What level of depth or complexity is appropriate?
- How should knowledge be structured and presented?

In other words, prompting externalises what was previously implicit in academic expertise.

Consider a familiar task: designing an exam question.

Traditionally, this would involve drawing on one's understanding of the subject, the learning objective and the level of students. With AI, the process becomes iterative and dialogic. A lecturer might begin with a broad prompt, refine it to increase analytical depth, adjust it to match assessment criteria, and generate multiple variations before selecting or adapting the most appropriate one. This aligns with emerging views of AI as supporting design exploration rather than simple task execution (Dwivedi et al., 2023).

The value here is not speed alone; it is the ability to explore a wider design space.

However, this expanded capability introduces a new responsibility. If poorly designed prompts can generate superficial or misaligned outputs, then effective academic use of AI depends not on the tool itself, but on the quality of intellectual framing provided by the user.

This is why prompt engineering, in an academic context, should not be treated as a technical skill alone. It is better understood as a form of scholarly practice – one that sits alongside writing, teaching, and research design.

This chapter builds on that premise. Rather than revisiting what prompts are, it focuses on how they can be used to design:

- Research questions.
- Literature review and academic writing.
- Assessment design.
- Lecture content and learning experience.
- Learning experiences.

In doing so, it shifts the conversation from using AI to thinking with AI in academically meaningful ways.

3. PROMPT ENGINEERING AS ACADEMIC DESIGN PRACTICE

To fully appreciate the role of prompt engineering in academia, it is useful to reconsider what academics actually do. At its core, academic work is not simply about generating content. It is about framing problems, structuring inquiry, guiding interpretation, and evaluating understanding.

These are fundamentally design activities.

When a lecturer prepares a session, they are not merely presenting information; they are designing a pathway through which students encounter and make sense of concepts. When a researcher formulates a question, they are not just asking something – they are defining the boundaries of knowledge production. Generating such materials can be time-consuming, especially when instructors aim to create examples that are relevant to contemporary organisational contexts.

LLMs can assist in this process by helping instructors generate illustrative scenarios, discussion questions, or case-based examples that make abstract concepts more tangible for students.

Prompt engineering intersects with this design work in a powerful way. A well-crafted prompt does more than instruct a model. It encodes:

- Assumptions about the topic.
- Expectations about the output.
- Implicit criteria for quality.

LLMs are highly sensitive to contextual cues embedded within prompts (Wei et al., 2022). For example, compare the following prompts:

> *Generate questions on organisational behaviour.*

and

> *Generate three analytical essay questions on organisational behaviour that require students to apply theory to real-world organisational challenges.*

The difference is not merely linguistic. The second prompt reflects a deeper engagement with:

- The purpose of the task (assessment).
- The level of cognition required (analysis and application).
- The context in which knowledge is used (real-world challenges).

Imagine a lecturer teaching a session on transformational leadership in an organisational behaviour course. Instead of relying solely on textbook examples, the lecturer might prompt the model as follows:

> *Create a short classroom scenario that illustrates transformational leadership in a modern organisation. The example should show how a leader inspires employees during a period of organisational change.*

The resulting scenario might describe a leader motivating a team during digital transformation or organisational restructuring. The lecturer can then adapt this example, refine it, or transform it into a discussion exercise.

Prompting can also support the development of interactive classroom activities. For instance:

> *Design a classroom discussion exercise that helps undergraduate students understand the difference between transactional and transformational leadership.*

Such prompts can generate ideas for debates, role-playing activities, or reflective exercises that encourage students to engage more actively with course material. Importantly, these generated ideas are not intended to replace the instructor's pedagogical judgement. Instead, they function as creative starting points that instructors can adopt to their specific learning objectives.

Instructors can also use prompting to tailor explanations for different levels of learners. Explaining a concept to undergraduate students often requires a different level of abstraction than explaining the same concept to doctoral researchers. Prompts can therefore specify the intended audience, such as:

> *Explain institutional theory in a way that first-year undergraduate business students can understand. Use simple organisational examples.*

This type of prompt encourages the model to simplify terminologies and use relatable examples, making the explanation more accessible to novice learners.

Educational researchers increasingly note that Gen AI tools can support instructional design and pedagogical creativity when used thoughtfully (Kasneci et al., 2023). However, they also emphasise that the effectiveness of such tools depends on the educator's ability to critically evaluate and refine the generated content.

Ultimately, prompting can help lecturers experiment with new ways of presenting material, designing activities, and illustrating complex ideas. Rather than replacing the educator's role, it provides a flexible tool that can expand the range of pedagogical possibilities available to instructors.

In this sense, prompt engineering becomes an act of pedagogical and intellectual intentionality.

3.1. From Content Creation to Design Exploration

One of the most significant advantages of using AI in academic work is the ability to generate multiple alternatives quickly.

In traditional workflows, generating one high-quality exam question or case study can take considerable time. As a result, academics often work with a limited set of options. Prompt engineering changes this dynamic by enabling rapid iteration.

For instance, a lecturer might:

- Generate 10 variations of a case-based questions.
- Compare their levels of complexity.
- Select or combine elements from different outputs.

This process mirrors design thinking more than traditional writing. It is exploratory, iterative, and comparative rather than linear.

However, this also raises an important point: more output does not automatically mean better design and quality (Amershi et al., 2019).

Without a clear framework for evaluation, the abundance of generated content can become overwhelming or even counterproductive. Academics must therefore develop the ability to:

- Recognise what constitutes a strong question or explanation.
- Identify gaps or inaccuracies.
- Refine outputs in line with learning objectives.

In other words, prompt engineering does not eliminate judgement; it amplifies the need for it.

3.2. The Invisible Layer: Making Expertise Explicit

A less visible but more profound shift introduced by prompt engineering is the need to articulate what was previously intuitive.

Experienced academics often rely on tacit knowledge when designing teaching materials or research questions. They 'know' what a good question looks like but may not always be able to fully articulate why.

Prompting disrupts this tacit process.

To generate a useful output, the academic must specify:

- The level of students.
- The type of question.
- The expected depth of response.
- The context or application.

This act of specification makes expertise more explicit. It forces the academic to translate intuition into clear, communicable criteria, where externalisation of tacit knowledge is seen as a key step in reflective practice (Zawacki-Richter et al., 2019).

Over time, this can have a reflective benefit. By repeatedly designing and refining prompts, academics may develop a more conscious understanding of their own pedagogical and research practices.

3.3. Bridging Design and Evaluation

A recurring theme across this chapter will be the relationship between design and evaluation. In Chapter 2, we discussed criteria such as accuracy, relevance, and depth. In this chapter, these criteria take on a more applied role within academic work.

When generating outputs using AI, academics are not merely asking 'what can the model produce?' but 'how well does this output serve a specific intellectual purpose?' This requires continuous evaluating of judgement. For instance:

- *When generating research questions*: Are they meaningful, theoretically grounded, and capable of advancing inquiry?
- *When designing assessment items*: Do they align with learning outcomes and levels of cognitive engagement?
- *When preparing lecture content*: Does it support conceptual understanding rather than surface-level coverage?

Evaluation, therefore, is not a separate step that follows generation; it is embedded within the design process. To make this explicit, prompt engineering, therefore, should not be seen as a linear activity (write prompt → get output) but as a cyclical and iterative practice which includes five clear interrelated stages: define, design, generate, evaluate, and refine (Fig. 29).

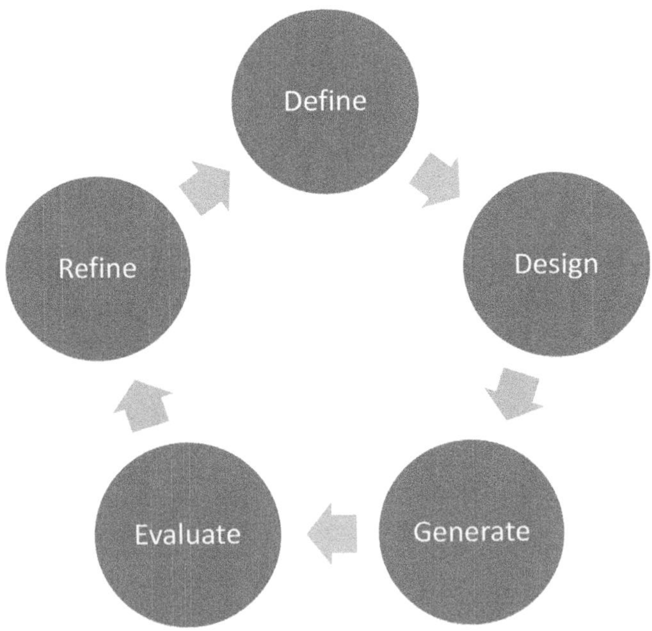

Fig. 29. Cyclical Process of Prompt Engineering.

Academic expertise is more visible in this cycle. Each stage serves a distinct function:

- *Define*: Clarify the intellectual goal (e.g., generating research questions, structuring a lecture, and synthesising literature).
- *Design*: Construct the prompt by specifying context, constraints, and the desired form of output.
- *Generate*: Engage the model to produce an initial response.
- *Evaluate*: Assess the output using criteria such as accuracy, relevance, depth, and alignment with purpose.
- *Refine*: Modify the prompt or the framing of the task based on this evaluation.

Crucially, this cycle is not completed once; it is repeated, often multiple times, until the output reaches a level of conceptual and practical adequacy.

What distinguishes expert use from novice use is not the ability to write a single effective prompt, but the ability to navigate this cycle deliberately. Academic expertise becomes most visible in:

- How the problem is *defined.*
- How constraints are *introduced.*
- How outputs are *interrogated* and *refined.*

In this sense, prompt engineering is less about eliciting answers and more about structuring an iterative process of thinking. Below, we will see how to apply the cyclical process (Fig. 29) with the help of some examples.

One of the earliest and most intuitive uses of this cycle is for conceptual clarification. Scholars frequently encounter unfamiliar ideas when reading outside their immediate area of expertise, reviewing interdisciplinary literature, or preparing new teaching materials. In such a situation, prompting can function as an exploratory tool that helps users orient themselves within a new intellectual landscape, but only when used iteratively.

Consider a lecturer preparing a new module on digital organisations who encounters the concept of algorithmic management. A novice interaction might begin and end with:

> *Explain algorithmic management.*

This reflects a single-pass interaction (write prompt → get output), with minimal evaluation or refinement. In contrast, a more productive prompt follows the full cycle:

Define:

The goal is not just definition but conceptual grounding and critical awareness.

Design:

'Explain the concept of algorithmic management in organisations. Describe its key characteristics, its relevance to platform-based work and some of the debates surrounding its impact on workers.'

Generate:

The model produces a structured response.

Evaluate:

The lecturer assesses:

- Is the explanation conceptually accurate?
- Are key debates represented or oversimplified?
- Is anything important missing (e.g., power asymmetries, surveillance concerns, etc.)?

Refine:

Follow-up prompts deepen the inquiry:

- 'Expand on critiques of algorithmic management from a labour process perspective.'
- 'How does algorithmic management relate to issues of worker autonomy and control?'

Through this iterative engagement, the interaction shifts from information retrieval to structured sensemaking.

Importantly, the model is not replacing academic reading. Rather, it acts as an orientation device, helping the user map the conceptual terrain before engaging with primary sources. This aligns with observations that LLMs are particularly useful in early-stage sensemaking within unfamiliar domains (Dwivedi et al., 2023). The same cyclical logic applies when distinguishing between related constructs, which is often necessary in both teaching and research. For example, a researcher exploring organisational identity might wish to clarify the distinction between organisational culture and organisational climate. A prompt such as the following encourages analytical comparison:

Design (initial prompt):

'Compare organisational culture and organisational climate. Explain how these concepts differ in terms of their theoretical foundations, measurement approaches, and implications for organisational research.'

Evaluate:

Does the output:

- Capture foundational differences (e.g., deep assumptions vs perceptual states)?
- Distinguish methodological approaches clearly?
- Avoid collapsing the concepts into superficial similarities?

Refine:

- 'Provide examples of how each concept is operationalized in empirical research.'
- 'What are the implications of confusing these constructs in organizational studies?'

Here again, understanding emerges not from a single response, but from iterative refinement guided by evaluation. Responses generated through such prompts can help scholars recognise differences in emphasis, methodology, and interpretation within existing scholarship.

However, scholars must remain attentive to the limitations of AI-generated explanations. As language models rely on patterns learned from training data rather than direct knowledge verification, their outputs may sometimes simplify complex debates or omit important nuances. Researchers therefore emphasise the importance of critical evaluation and cross-checking with peer-reviewed literature (Bender et al., 2021).

In practice, the most effective use of prompting for conceptual exploration involves a dialogic process; rather than accepting the first answer produced by the model, users can ask follow-up questions, request clarifications, or challenge aspects of the explanation. Through this iterative dialogue, prompting becomes less about obtaining answers and more about refining understanding through interaction.

3.4. Towards a Practice-oriented Use of AI

What emerges from this discussion is a shift in orientation. Instead of asking:

> *How can I get the best output from AI?*

Academics begin to ask:

> *How can I use AI to design better intellectual experiences for students and stronger foundations for research?*

This shift is subtle but transformative.

It moves AI from the periphery of academic work to its core – not as a replacement for thinking, but as a medium through which thinking is explored, tested, and refined.

4. DESIGNING RESEARCH QUESTIONS WITH AI: FROM IDEA GENERATION TO SCHOLARLY FRAMING

Most academics don't struggle with having topics. They struggle with finding the right question within those topics. If there is one aspect of academic work where the promise (and limitation) of Gen AI becomes immediately visible, it is in the formulation of research questions.

Research questions are not merely procedural starting points; they are epistemic commitments. They define what counts as knowledge, what is worth investigating, and how inquiry is to be structured (Creswell & Creswell, 2018). A poorly framed question can lead to trivial findings, while a well-crafted one can open entirely new avenues of understanding.

At first glance, using AI to generate research questions feels almost effortless. You type:

> *Generate research questions on employee engagement.*

Within seconds, you receive a list. It looks polished. It sounds academic and it also feels productive.

But if you pause and read carefully, something feels off.

The questions are:

- Familiar.
- Predictable.
- Already asked in slightly different ways.

This is not a limitation of the model alone. It is a reflection of how the prompt was framed. As research on LLMs reminds us, these systems are designed to produce plausible continuations, not necessarily novel insights. This reflects a broader concern raised in discussions on Gen AI: that fluency of output may be mistaken for intellectual depth (Bender et al., 2021).

The value of prompt engineering, therefore, lies not in asking AI 'generate research questions', but in using it to support the intellectual work of refining, situating, and interrogating those questions. So, the real question is not: *can LLMs generate research questions?* It clearly can. The more useful question is: *how do we use LLMs to arrive at better questions than we would have otherwise?* In such moments, prompting can function as a form of structured brainstorming.

Strong research questions rarely emerge from topics alone. They emerge from tensions, contradictions, and gaps within existing knowledge (Alvesson & Sandberg, 2011). AI does not automatically *see* these tensions. But it can help you explore them if you make them visible in your prompt.

Let's revisit the earlier example.

Initial prompt:

> *Generate research questions on employee engagement.*

Typical output (simplified)

- What factors influence employee engagement?
- How does leadership affect engagement?
- What is the relationship between engagement and performance?

There is nothing wrong here. But there is nothing particularly insightful either. Now consider a revised prompt:

> *Generate research questions on employee engagement that explore tensions between organisational performance metrics and employee well-being in hybrid work settings.*

Notice what has changed. This prompt introduces:

- A conceptual tension (performance vs well-being).
- A contextual boundary (hybrid work).
- A direction for enquiry.

The output will now begin to shift as the prompt is more structured.

To make this usable, it helps to think of prompt design for research questions in three parts:

- Tension – what is the conflict, gap, or contradiction?
- Context – where is this happening?
- Lens – through which concept or theory are you examining it?

For example:

Generate research questions on employee voice (topic)

Focusing on tensions between surveillance and autonomy tension)

In AI-enabled workplaces (context)

Using an organizational justice perspective (lens).

This simple structure immediately elevates the quality of output.

More importantly, the researcher can then refine the conversation by introducing additional context:

Suggest research questions that examine employee voice in organisations using AI-driven monitoring systems.

Through this process, prompting becomes a way of exploring conceptual possibilities rather than producing ready-made research designs.

4.1. Designing for Qualitative Inquiry: Depth, Experience, and Meaning

Qualitative research is particularly sensitive to how questions are framed, as it seeks to uncover meanings, experiences, and processes rather than measurable relationships (Corbin & Strauss, 2015).

When using AI to generate qualitative research questions, the risk is that outputs become overly general or descriptive rather than interpretive. For example:

How do employees experience remote work?

The output can be overly simplistic without any critical gap.

To counter this, prompts must signal:

- Interpretive intent.
- Conceptual anchors.
- Sensitivity to context.

For example:

> *Generate qualitative research questions exploring how employees construct their professional identity in long-term remote work environments, with attention to belonging, visibility and boundary management.*

Such a prompt does more than specify a topic. It embeds:

- Theoretical constructs (identity, belonging).
- Process orientation (construction).
- Lived experience dimension (visibility, boundaries).

This process raises questions that are not only richer but also more aligned with qualitative epistemology.

At this stage, AI becomes less of a generator and more of a thinking partner – helping the researcher explore how different conceptual lenses might shape the inquiry.

4.2. Designing for Quantitative Inquiry: Precision and Structure

Quantitative research, in contrast, requires clarity, operationalisation, and a focus on relationships between variables (Creswell & Creswell, 2018). Here, the challenge is different. AI can generate variable-based questions relatively easily, but these may lack:

- Theoretical grounding.
- Clarity in measurement.
- Awareness of methodological feasibility.

A prompt such as: 'Generate quantitative research questions on remote work and productivity' may produce relationships, but they remain under-specified. A more academically useful prompt would be:

> *Generate quantitative research questions examining the relationship between remote work intensity and employee productivity, including potential mediating variables such as job autonomy and moderating variables such as organisational support.*

This prompt introduces:

- Clear independent and dependent variables.
- Analytical sophistication (mediation, moderation).
- Alignment with empirical research design.

What emerges is not just a question, but the outline of a research model. However, it is important to note that AI does not validate whether these relationships are theoretically meaningful or empirically viable. This remains the responsibility of the researchers.

4.3. Iterative Refinement: Where Real Value Emerges

Perhaps the most underappreciated use of AI in research design is not initial generation, but iterative refinement.

A researcher might begin with a broad prompt but then progressively narrow and deepen the inquiry:

- 'Refine these research questions to align with institutional theory.'
- 'Identify potential gaps in these questions based on recent literature.'
- 'Refine these questions to focus on emerging economies.'

This process reflects what Alvesson and Sandberg (2011) describe as problematisation – the questioning of underlying assumptions within existing research. Through this process, AI supports a form of dialogic thinking, where the researcher engages in a structured exploration of possibilities.

Importantly, this iterative engagement can surface:

- Hidden assumptions.
- Overlooked variables.
- Alternative theoretical perspectives.

However, the quality of refinement depends on the researcher's ability to guide the conversation. Without this, iteration risks becoming a circular, redundant, and superficial process rather than progressive.

4.4. From Plausibility to Originality: A Critical Tension

A key limitation of AI-generated research questions lies in their tendency towards plausibility rather than originality.

Because models are trained on existing knowledge, they are more likely to reproduce dominant themes than to identify genuinely novel gaps. This can lead to questions that are:

- Well-phrased.
- Methodologically sound.
- But intellectually unremarkable.

For academics, this is a critical point of reflection.

AI can assist in structuring ideas, exploring variations, and identifying common patterns. But it cannot replace the creative and critical insight required to identify meaningful research problems.

In this sense, prompt engineering should be used to:

- Expand the range of possibilities.
- Test alternative framings.
- Clarify thinking.

But to outsource the core intellectual task of inquiry.

4.5. Using AI to Stress-test Research Questions

An underutilised but highly valuable application of AI is in evaluating and stress-testing research questions. For example:

> *Critically evaluate the following research question in terms of clarity, originality and feasibility.*

Or

> *What are the potential limitations of this research question?*

This shifts AI from a generative role to a critical role.

While the feedback must be interpreted cautiously, it can help researchers to identify ambiguities, recognise overbroad scope, and anticipate methodological challenges. In this way, AI contributes not just to the creation of questions but to their refinement and strengthening.

4.6. A Reflective Pause

At this stage, it becomes evident that the value of AI in research design is not in producing ready-made questions but in supporting a more reflective and iterative process of inquiry.

The researcher remains central:

- As the originator of ideas.
- As the evaluator of outputs.
- As the arbiter of what constitutes meaningful research.

Prompt engineering, when used thoughtfully, does not simplify these roles. It makes them more explicit.

In the next section, we talk about assessment design using LLMs. If research questions represent the starting point of academic inquiry, assessments represent its evaluation. Prompt engineering has an immediate and tangible impact on assessment design which is rigorous, aligned, and pedagogically meaningful.

5. LITERATURE EXPLORATION AND ACADEMIC WRITING WITH AI

If teaching and assessment shape how knowledge is transmitted, engagement with literature and scholarly writing defines how knowledge is constructed, challenged, and extended. For academics and researchers, this is not a peripheral activity – it is the core of intellectual work.

Yet this is also where the use of LLMs becomes most contested.

On the surface, the application seems straightforward. A researcher might ask:

> *Write a literature review on algorithmic bias in HR.*

The result will be competent, fluent, structured, and readable. It may even reference familiar debates like fairness concerns, recruitment algorithms, and regulatory debates.

But something crucial is missing.

The output is competent but does not advance understanding. It summarises what is already visible rather than helping the researchers see differently.

Now consider a different approach:

> *I am writing a theory building paper on algorithmic bias in hiring systems. Map the literature into three streams: technical bias detection, organisational consequences and regulatory ethics. For each stream, identify its central assumption and an unresolved tension. Do not summarise articles; synthesise patterns.*

Notice what changed.

The second prompt does not merely request content. It defines purpose, structure, and intellectual ambition.

It tells the model how to think, not what to retrieve.

It introduces:

- A purpose (theory building).
- A structure (three streams).
- An intellectual task (identifying tensions).

This distinction echoes research on few-shot learning by Brown et al. (2020), which showed that large models infer task structure from contextual cues. Later studies on chain-of-thought (CoT) prompting (Wei et al. 2022) demonstrated that reasoning improves dramatically when models are guided through intermediate steps.

The introduction of Gen AI into this space has generated both excitement and unease. On the other hand, AI can assist in summarising articles, suggesting themes and structuring arguments. On the other hand, it raises serious concerns regarding accuracy, originality, and epistemic reliability. This section takes a balanced view. Rather than asking whether AI should or should not be used in academic writing, the focus here is on how it can be used responsibly to support rather than dilute scholarly thinking.

5.1. From Information Retrieval to Sensemaking

Traditionally, engaging with literature involves a sequence of activities like searching for relevant sources, reading and annotating texts, identifying themes and gaps, and synthesising insights. AI has the potential to accelerate parts of this process, particularly in summarisation and initial exploration. A prompt such as: 'Summarise the key arguments in institutional theory' can produce a quick overview. However, this convenience introduces a subtle but important shift – from sensemaking to consumption.

Summaries generated by AI often prioritise coherence over nuance, flatten competing perspectives, and omit methodological and contextual details.

As a result, while they may be useful as starting points, they cannot substitute for direct engagement and primary sources. They create the illusion of understanding without the depth.

A more productive use of AI is to support sensemaking, rather than replace it. For example:

> *I am conducting a literature review on institutional theory within organisational research. Compare how different scholars*

conceptualise institutional change, highlighting key differences in assumptions and focus.

This type of prompt encourages comparison, contrast, and analytical framing. It can also help in identifying keywords, alternative terms, etc. Even here, however, the output must be treated as provisional, requiring verification against actual texts.

5.2. Mapping a Field: Identifying Themes and Gaps

One of the more promising applications of AI is in helping researchers map a field of study. For instance:

Identify major themes in recent research on digital transformation in organisations.

This can generate thematic clusters, recurring concepts, and emerging areas of interest. Such outputs can be useful in the early stages of a project, helping researchers orient themselves within a body of literature.

However, there are two important limitations. First, AI does not have an up-to-date or complete understanding of the literature. Its outputs are shaped by training data, which may not reflect the most recent publications and niche or emerging debates.

Second, AI tends to reproduce dominant narratives. Less visible perspectives or critical viewpoints may be underrepresented. To address this, prompts can be refined to explicitly seek diversity:

Identify dominant and underexplored themes in research on digital transformation from arXiv, including critical perspectives.

The second prompt actively pushes against bias in the output by augmenting the prompt on where to look and what to look. Even then, the researcher must actively verify and extend these insights through attentive literature review.

5.3. Multiple Perspectives

Researchers can use prompting to examine ideas from different theoretical perspectives. For instance:

How might institutional theory explain the adoption of remote work policies in organisations?

Followed by:

> *How might resource dependence theory explain the same phenomenon?*

By comparing these responses, the researcher may gain insight into how different theoretical frameworks emphasise distinct causal mechanisms. This type of exploration can be particularly useful during the early stages of research design when scholars are evaluating alternative conceptual approaches.

Nevertheless, scholars should approach AI-generated research suggestions with caution. Generative models are capable of producing plausible ideas, but they do not possess genuine understanding of research gaps, methodological feasibility, or theoretical significance. As a result, the responsibility for evaluating the novelty and rigour of research ideas remains firmly with the researcher.

Recent studies on Gen AI in scientific work emphasise that such systems should be viewed as tools for cognitive augmentation rather than autonomous research assistants (Gilson et al., 2024). When used appropriately, prompting can help scholars reflect on ideas, test assumptions, and explore conceptual alternatives. Yet the intellectual responsibility for developing robust research remains a human endeavour.

5.4. The Risk of Fabrication: A Critical Warning

One of the most significant challenges in using AI for literature work is the phenomenon often referred to as hallucination, as discussed in Chapter 2. It refers to the generation of information that appears credible but is not factually accurate (Bender et al., 2021).

In the context of academic writing, this can take the form of:

- Fabricated citation.
- Misattributed ideas.
- Incorrect summaries.

This is not a minor limitation; it is a fundamental constraint. As a result, AI should never be relied upon as a source of citations. Instead, it should be used to generate ideas, suggest directions, and support structuring. All references must be verified through academic databases, primary sources, and peer-reviewed literature. This reinforces a broader principle:

> *AI can assist with thinking, but it cannot be treated as an authority on knowledge.*

5.5. Structuring Arguments: From Ideas to Coherent Narratives

One of the most constructive uses of AI in academic writing lies in structuring arguments.

Researchers often struggle not with ideas, but with organising those ideas into a coherent narrative. Prompt engineering can support this process. For example:

> *Create an outline for a literature review on employee well-being in a hybrid work setting, including key themes and logical progression.*

This can help in organising sections, identifying connections between ideas, and ensuring flow. But the real value emerges when prompts move beyond structure into arguments:

> *Suggest ways to structure an argument/literature review that critiques existing research on algorithmic bias, highlighting gaps and tensions.*

This encourages:

- Critical positioning.
- Identification of gaps.
- Development of a narrative arc.

However, there is a subtle risk. AI-generated structures often follow conventional patterns, which may limit originality. While these structures provide clarity, they should not constrain the researcher's ability to develop novel arguments.

5.6. Writing Support: Clarity, Not Substitution

AI can also assist with aspects of writing such as paraphrasing, improving clarity, and refining tone. For instance:

> *Rewrite this paragraph to improve clarity while maintaining an academic tone.*

This can be particularly helpful for:

- Non-native English speaker.
- Early-career researchers.
- Interdisciplinary scholars.

However, it is important to distinguish between support and substitution. When AI is used to clarify expression or refine language, it enhances communication. But when it is used to generate entire sections or produce arguments without critical engagement, it risks undermining intellectual ownership. Academic writing is not merely about producing text – it is about developing and expressing original thought. This cannot be outsourced.

5.7. Iterative Dialogue: AI as a Thinking Partner

One of the most valuable ways to use AI in writing is through iterative dialogue. A researcher might propose an argument, ask for critique, refine the idea, and test alternative framings. For example:

> *Critique this argument on the ethical implications of AI in hiring.*

Or

> *What are potential counterarguments to this position?*

Or

> *For each major stream in algorithmic bias research, identify its central assumption and one unresolved tension or contradiction.*

This process can reveal weaknesses, surface assumptions, or/and strengthen reasoning. Importantly, this mirrors the kind of intellectual exchange that occurs in:

- Peer review.
- Academic discussion.
- Collaborative research.

Across these examples, one theme becomes clear: effective prompting in academic contexts resembles a dialogue rather than a command. Scholars do not simply issue instructions to obtain final answers. Instead, they engage in iterative conversations that gradually refine understanding and generate insights.

This dialogic perspective reflects broader discussions about how humans interact with intelligent systems. Researchers studying human–AI collaboration note that the most productive interactions occur when users treat AI outputs as provisional contributions that require interpretation and refinement (Amershi et al., 2019).

For academics, this mindset is particularly important. Scholarship depends not only on producing information but also on interpreting evidence, questioning assumptions, and engaging with competing perspectives. Prompting therefore works best when it is integrated into these existing scholarly practices rather than used as a shortcut to bypass them.

Unlike static tools, LLMs allow for back-and-forth interaction. A researcher can:

- Ask for initial research questions.
- Request refinement based on a theoretical framework.
- Challenge the assumptions embedded in the output.
- Explore alternative perspectives.

This iterative dialogue resembles scholarly inquiry itself.

However, it is important to recognise that the 'dialogue' is asymmetric. The AI does not possess understanding in the human sense; it generates responses based on patterns in data. The responsibility for direction, critique, and validation remains with the user.

This reinforces a central argument of this chapter:

> *AI extends academic capability but does not replace academic responsibility.*

Seen in this light, prompting becomes less about mastering technical tricks and more about cultivating a reflective approach to interacting with generative technologies. The scholar remains at the centre of the process, guiding the direction of inquiry, and evaluating the quality of the ideas that emerge.

AI, in this sense, becomes a simulated interlocutor – not replacing scholarly dialogue, but supplementing it.

5.8. A Reflective Pause

Across this section, a consistent theme emerges that AI can accelerate exploration, enhance clarity, and support structuring. But it cannot replace deep reading, critical thinking, and original insight. For academics, the challenge is not whether to use AI but how to integrate it in a way that strengthens rather than diminishes scholarly practice.

Institutions are still developing guidelines in this area, but a general principle can be articulated as:

> *AI may assist in the process of writing, but the intellectual contribution must remain the author's own.*

Having examined research design, assessment, teaching, and writing, we now arrive at the final step of bringing these elements together into a coherent academic workflow.

The concluding section will synthesise these insights and provide a practical framework for integrating prompt engineering into everyday academic work.

6. DESIGNING ASSESSMENTS USING AI: FROM QUESTION GENERATION TO PEDAGOGICAL INTENT

Assessment is one of the most consequential aspects of academic practice. It is through assessment that we signal what matters, what counts as knowledge, and how deeply students are expected to engage with a subject. In this sense, assessment is not simply a mechanism for evaluation; it is a design activity that shapes learning itself.

The introduction of Gen AI into this space brings both opportunity and risk. On the one hand, prompt engineering allows academics to generate a wide range of assessment materials quickly, like multiple-choice questions, essay prompts, case-based scenarios, and even entire assessment structures. On the other hand, this ease of generation raises an important concern: does speed compromise pedagogical intent?

The central arguments of this section are that LLMs can enhance assessment design only when they are used not as a shortcut but as a tool for exploring and refining pedagogical choices. LLMs can be used to generate assessments that can align with learning objectives, can control cognitive level, embed real-world scenarios, and generate variations to suit the audience's needs (Fig. 30).

We will discuss the above utility depicted in Fig. 30 in the below sections.

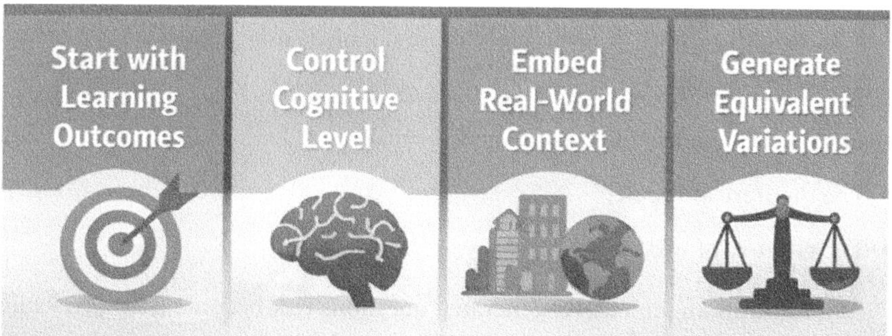

Fig. 30. Techniques for Designing Assessment Using LLMs.

6.1. Assessment as Alignment with Learning Objectives, Not Output (Questions)

Before engaging with prompts, it is important to return to a foundational principle in higher education: constructive alignment (Biggs, 1996). According to this framework, effective assessment must align with:

- Intended learning outcomes.
- Teaching activities.
- Levels of cognitive engagement.

This has a direct implication for prompt engineering. A prompt that generates an assessment item is only useful if it reflects this alignment.

Consider the below prompt:

> *Create questions on leadership.*

This bypasses pedagogy entirely.

Instead, use a learning-outcome-first prompt structure.

Prompt template:

- Define module/topic.
- Specify learning outcomes.
- Define cognitive level.

Example:

> *I am teaching a postgraduate course on leadership. Students should be able to critically apply transformational and transactional leadership theories to real organisational contexts. Design assessment questions aligned with this outcome.*

The second prompt is not merely more detailed; it is aligned with a learning objective. It signals:

- The level of cognition (critical application).
- The theoretical focus.
- The context of use.

Without this alignment, AI-generated questions risk becoming academically disconnected, even if they appear well-structured. The latter reflects alignment with higher-order cognitive skills, consistent with Bloom's taxonomy (Anderson & Krathwohl, 2001).

6.2. Designing Across Cognitive Levels

One of the most powerful applications of prompt engineering in assessment design lies in its ability to generate questions across different levels of cognitive complexity. Academics often intend to access higher-order thinking but end up testing recall.

In traditional practice, academics often rely on implicit judgement to vary question difficulty. AI makes this variation more explicit and more controllable.

For example:

> *Create three questions on motivation theory: one testing basic understanding, one requiring application, and one requiring critical evaluation.*

Or

> *Design one question each that tests analysis, synthesis and evaluation in the context of organisational change.*

The outputs generated through such a prompt can help lecturers visualise how the same topic can be approached at different depths. It makes cognitive expectations visible and helps balance difficulty across assessments.

More importantly, this process encourages reflection on an often-overlooked question:

> *Are we assessing what we intend students to learn, or merely what is easy to test?*

By deliberately designing prompts that target different cognitive levels (Biggs & Tang, 2011), academics can ensure that assessments move beyond recall towards analysis, synthesis, and evaluation.

6.3. From Generic to Contextualised Assessment

A common limitation of AI-generated questions is their tendency to remain decontextualised. While such questions may test conceptual understanding, they often fail to capture the complexity of real-world application.

Prompt engineering can address this by embedding context directly into the task.

For instance:

> *Design a case-based question where students must apply stakeholder theory to a multinational company facing ethical challenges in its supply chain.*

This prompt introduces:

- A realistic organisational context.
- An applied theoretical lens.
- An implicit requirement for judgement and reasoning.

The resulting question is not only more engaging but also more aligned with contemporary pedagogical emphasis on authentic assessment (Boud & Falchikov, 2007).

Authentic assessments are particularly important in disciplines such as business, management, and the social sciences, where students are expected to apply knowledge in complex and often ambiguous situations. AI can support this by generating:

- Scenarios.
- Stakeholder perspectives.
- Decision-making dilemmas.

However, these outputs should be treated as draft material, requiring refinement to ensure relevance and realism.

6.4. Designing Multiple Pathways: Variation and Fairness

Another area where LLMs can significantly enhance assessment design is generating multiple versions of similar questions. This has practical implications for large cohorts, academic integrity, and formative practice.

For example:

> *Generate five variations of a question assessing organisational culture, each using a different industry context.*

This allows lecturers to:

- Maintain consistency in learning outcomes.

- Introduce variation in context.
- Reduce predictability in assessment.

At a deeper level, this capability supports a more nuanced approach to fairness. Rather than assuming that a signal question works equally well for all students, academics can design parallel tasks that accommodate different ways of engaging with material.

However, this also requires careful oversight. Variation must not lead to unequal difficulty levels, and generated questions must be reviewed for consistency.

6.5. The Role of Feedback in AI-generated Assessment

Assessment is incomplete without feedback. Yet, designing meaningful feedback is often more time-consuming than designing the assessment itself. AI can assist in generating:

- Model answers.
- Marking rubrics.
- Indicative feedback comments.

For instance:

> *Provide a model answer and making rubric for the following essay questions on organisational ethics that distinguishes between excellent, good and weak responses.*

This can serve as a starting point for developing:

- Clearer grading standards.
- More consistent evaluation.
- Transparent expectations for students.

However, there is an important caveat. AI-generated feedback often tends towards generic clarity rather than pedagogical nuance. It may explain what is correct, but not always why a student's reasoning is strong or weak in a specific context. As Nicol and Macfarlane-Dick (2006) argue, effective feedback supports self-regulation, not just correctness.

Therefore, AI should be seen as supporting the structure of feedback, while the academic remains responsible for its interpretive depth.

6.6. Designing Assessment for Learning, Not Just Evaluation

One of the most significant risks in using AI for assessment design is that it reinforces a narrow view of assessment as a tool for measurement.

In contrast, contemporary educational theory emphasises assessment for learning (Boud & Falchikov, 2007; Nicol & Macfarlane-Dick, 2006), where assessment itself becomes a learning activity.

Prompt engineering can support this shift by enabling the design of:

- Practice questions with feedback.
- Reflective prompts.
- Iterative assignments.

For example:

> *Design a formative assessment where students analyse a failed organisational change initiative and reflect on what could have been done differently.*

Such tasks encourage:

- Critical thinking.
- Self-reflection.
- Application of theory.

In this context, AI is not just generating questions; it is supporting the design of learning experiences.

6.7. Risks and Boundaries in AI-generated Assessment

Despite its potential, the use of AI in assessment design must be approached with caution.

One concern is the risk of homogenisation. If multiple educators rely on similar prompts, there is a possibility that assessments become standardised in unintended ways, reducing diversity in academic evaluation.

Another concern relates to bias. AI-generated scenarios or examples may reflect implicit assumptions that disadvantage certain groups or perspectives. This requires careful review and, where necessary, deliberate correction.

A further issue is the illusion of quality. Well-written questions are not necessarily good questions. They may appear sophisticated while lacking alignment with learning outcomes or failing to elicit meaningful responses. These risks highlight a central principle:

AI can assist in generating assessment material, but it cannot determine what constitutes good assessment.

That judgement remains inherently academic.

6.8. A Reflective Pause

At this point, it becomes clear that the role of prompt engineering in assessment design is not to automate the process but to expand the space of possibilities within which academics make decisions.

It allows lecturers to:

- Explore alternative question designs.
- Test different levels of difficulty.
- Generate diverse contexts.

But the final responsibility – to ensure alignment, fairness, and intellectual value – remains firmly with the academic.

In the next section, we move from assessment to learning design. If assessment defines how learning is evaluated, lectures and classroom activities shape how learning unfolds. In the next section, we extend this discussion by examining how prompt engineering can support the design of engaging, structured, and inclusive learning experiences.

7. DESIGNING LECTURE CONTENT AND LEARNING EXPERIENCES WITH AI

If assessment determines what is evaluated, lectures and classroom experiences shape how knowledge is encountered, interpreted, and internalised (Laurillard, 2012). For many academics, lecture preparation is an iterative and time-intensive process which requires balancing conceptual clarity, engagement, pacing, and relevance.

Gen AI introduces a new possibility into this process: the ability to rapidly prototype and reconfigure learning experiences. However, as with assessment design, the value of AI lies not in producing ready-made content but in supporting more thoughtful and varied design choices.

This section explores how prompt engineering can be used to enhance lecturer design not by replacing the lecturer's voice but by expanding the ways in which content can be structured, illustrated and experienced.

7.1. From Content Delivery to Learning Design

A useful starting point is to move away from thinking of lecturers as 'content delivery'. Contemporary pedagogy increasingly views lecturers as designers of learning experiences where students are guided through:

- Conceptual understanding.
- Application.
- Reflection.
- Interaction.

This shift has direct implications for prompt engineering. A prompt such as:

> *Explain organisational culture.*

Produces an explanation. But it does not produce a learning experience. In contrast:

> *Design a 90-minute lecture on organisational culture for postgraduate students, including key concepts, real-world examples, interactive activities and discussion questions.*

This prompt signals:

- Structure (time-bound session).
- Audience (postgraduate students).
- Pedagogical intent (interaction, application).

The difference is not in length but in design orientation. The second prompt treats AI not as a source of information, but as a collaborator in structuring learning. However, this will require a dialogic process to get effective lecture material. One prompt will not be enough.

7.2. Structuring Lectures: From Linear Flow to Layered Understanding

One of the most immediate uses of AI in lecture preparation is in generating structured outlines. For example:

> *Create a lecture outline on employee motivation that progresses from foundational theories to contemporary critiques, including examples and transitions between sections.*

Such prompts can help lecturers:

- Organise content logically.
- Ensure progression from simple to complex ideas.
- Identify gaps in coverage.

However, the real value lies in using AI to explore alternative structures. A lecturer might ask:

- 'Reframe this lecture using a problem-based approach.'
- 'Design the session around a central case study.'
- 'Structure this lecture as a debate between competing theories.'

This opens up different pedagogical possibilities:

- Linear explanation.
- Case-led exploration.
- Dialogic engagement.

Rather than settling for a single structure, academics can experiment with multiple ways of organising knowledge, selecting the one that best aligns with their teaching goals.

7.3. Generating Examples: Making Abstract Concepts Accessible

One of the most persistent challenges in teaching is translating abstract concepts into relatable and meaningful examples.

AI can be particularly useful here, as it can generate:

- Organisational scenarios.
- Everyday analogies.
- Cross-cultural illustrations.

For instance:

> *Provide real-world examples that illustrate the challenges of implementing diversity and inclusion initiatives in organisation.*

The outputs may include:

- Corporate case scenarios.
- Workplace dilemmas.
- Policy implementation challenges.

These examples can then be adapted, refined, or localised by the lecturer. However, an important consideration emerges. AI-generated examples often appear plausible, but they may lack:

- Contextual accuracy.
- Nuance.
- Relevance to specific student cohorts.

This reinforces the need for academic curation. The role of the lecturer is not to accept examples as given but to:

- Evaluate their appropriateness.
- Align them with learning objectives.
- Adapt them to the classroom context.

In this sense, AI supports the generation of examples, but the lecturer ensures their pedagogical value.

7.4. Designing Interaction: Moving Beyond Passive Learning

Perhaps the most significant opportunity offered by prompt engineering lies in designing interactive learning elements.

Traditional lecturers often rely heavily on one-way communication. However, research in higher education consistently emphasises the importance of active engagement for deeper learning.

AI can assist in designing:

- Discussion prompts.
- In-class activities.
- Reflective exercises.

For example:

> *Suggest classroom activities that help students critically engage with ethical dilemmas in AI-driven decision-making.*

This may generate:

- Small-group debates.
- Role-play scenarios.
- Decision-making exercises.

Similarly:

> *Create discussion questions that challenge students to compare different leadership theories in real-world contexts.*

Such prompts can produce questions that:

- Encourage multiple perspectives.
- Require application of theory.
- Stimulate dialogue.

However, it is important to recognise that interaction is not created by prompts alone. It is shaped by how activities are facilitated, how students are guided, and how discussions are framed.

AI can suggest possibilities, but the lecturer brings them to life.

7.5. Designing for Diverse Learners: Inclusivity and Accessibility

Classrooms are inherently diverse. Students differ in prior knowledge, learning styles, linguistic abilities, and cultural backgrounds. Designing lectures that accommodate this diversity is a complex task. Prompt engineering can support this by enabling lecturers to generate multiple representations of the same concept.

For instance:

> *Explain stakeholder theory in three ways: for a beginner, for an advanced student and using real-world business examples.*

This allows the lecture to:

- Scaffold learning.
- Provide layered explanations.
- Address different levels of understanding.

Similarly:

> *'Provide examples of organisational culture from different cultural contexts.'*

This can help avoid a narrow or culturally specific framing of concepts.

However, inclusivity requires more than variation. It requires critical awareness. AI-generated content may unintentionally reflect dominant cultural norms or biases (O'Neil, 2016). Academics must therefore actively review and adapt outputs to ensure that they:

- Represent diverse perspectives.
- Avoid stereotypes.
- Remain contextually appropriate.

7.6. Using AI for Reflection and Consolidation

Learning does not occur only through exposure to content; it requires reflection and consolidation. AI can assist in designing reflective prompts such as:

> *Create reflective questions that encourage students to connect motivation theory to their own work experiences.*

Or

> *Design a short activity where students evaluate the strengths and limitations of a theory discussed in class.*

These prompts support:

- Deeper engagement.
- Personal connection to material.
- Critical thinking.

They can be used:

- At the end of lectures.
- In online forums.
- As formative exercises.

In this way, AI contributes not just to the delivery of content but also to the internalisation of knowledge.

7.7. Balancing Efficiency and Authenticity

A recurring tension in using AI for lecture design is the balance between efficiency and authenticity. AI can significantly reduce the time required to generate outlines, create examples, and design activities.

However, there is a risk that lecturers become:

- Overly standardised.
- Detached from the lecturer's voice.
- Less responsive to specific classroom dynamics.

Students often value not just the content of a lecture but the perspective and experience of the lecturer. This cannot be generated through prompts. Therefore, AI should be used to:

- support preparation;
- expand possibilities;
- reduce routine workload;

but not to replace the distinctive intellectual and pedagogical identity of the academic.

7.8. A Reflective Pause

At this stage, a pattern becomes visible across research design, assessment, and lecture preparation. In each case, AI expands the range of options, accelerates generation, and supports iteration. But in each case, the academic remains responsible for selecting what matters, shaping how it is presented and ensuring its intellectual integrity.

Prompt engineering, therefore, does not simplify teaching. It reconfigures it as a more explicit design practice.

Having explored how AI can support the design of teaching and assessment, the next section turns to another critical dimension of academic work: engaging with literature and developing scholarly writing. Here, the opportunities are significant but so are the risks. We will explore them in the next section.

8. INTEGRATING PROMPT ENGINEERING INTO ACADEMIC PRACTICE

By this stage, prompt engineering has been explored across multiple domains of academic work – research design, assessment creation, lecture development, and scholarly writing. Each of these areas reveals a consistent pattern: Gen AI does not replace academic expertise; rather, it reshapes how that expertise is enacted.

The question that remains, therefore, is not what AI can do, but:

How can academics meaningfully integrate prompt engineering into their everyday practice without compromising intellectual rigour, pedagogical intent, or scholarly identity?

This final section addresses that question by moving from isolated use cases to a coherent academic workflow.

8.1. From Episodic Use to Embedded Practice

One of the most common ways in which academics currently engage with AI is episodic – using it occasionally to generate ideas, draft content, or explore a concept. While this can be useful, it often leads to inconsistent outcomes, limited learning about the tool itself, and underutilisation of its potential.

A more effective approach is to treat prompt engineering as an embedded practice – a routine part of how academic work is approached.

This does not mean using AI for everything. Rather, it involves identifying where AI adds value, where human judgement is essential or how the two can complement each other.

For instance:

- Using AI to generate multiple research question variations.
- But relying on scholarly judgement to select and refine the most meaningful one.

This shift from occasional use to intentional integration is what transforms AI from a novelty into a productive academic tool.

8.2. A Practical Workflow for Academics

To make this integration more tangible, it is useful to conceptualise prompt engineering as part of a cyclical workflow rather than a linear process.

A typical academic task, whether designing a lecture, developing an assessment, or writing a paper, can be approached through the following stages:

Exploration – At this stage, AI can be used to:

- Generate ideas.
- Map possibilities.
- Surface alternative perspectives.

Prompts here are typically open-ended, designed to expand the space of thinking.

Structuring – Once ideas are generated, the focus shifts to organisation. AI can assist in:

- Creating outlines.
- Grouping themes.
- Suggesting logical progression.

This stage benefits from more directed prompts that emphasise clarity and coherence.

Refinement – Here, the academic engages more critically with the material. AI can support:

- Rephrasing.
- Identifying gaps.
- Testing alternative framings.

However, this is also where human judgement becomes most central.

Evaluation – Finally, outputs are assessed in terms of:

- Accuracy.
- Relevance.
- Depth.

AI can play a role here as well, for instance, by offering critique, but the final evaluation must remain human-led.

Importantly, this process is iterative. Academics may move back and forth between stages, using prompts to refine their thinking at each step.

8.3. Developing Prompt Literacy

Just as academics develop methodological or theoretical expertise over time, effective use of AI requires the development of what might be termed prompt literacy. This involves:

- Understanding how prompts shape outputs.
- Recognising the limitations of generated responses.
- Knowing how to iterate effectively.

Prompt literacy is not about memorising techniques. It is about cultivating a way of thinking that is:

- Practice.
- Intentional.
- Reflective.

For example, an experienced user will:

- Anticipate how ambiguity in a prompt might lead to vague outputs.
- Recognise when additional context is needed.
- Know when to simplify rather than complicate a prompt.

Over time, this becomes an intuitive skill – much like designing a good research question or structuring a compelling argument.

8.4. Balancing Efficiency with Intellectual Integrity

One of the most significant benefits of AI is efficiency. As Floridi (2016) argues, the value of knowledge lies not in its production but in its validation and interpretation. Tasks that once took hours can now be completed in minutes with the help of LLMs via constructive and effective prompts.

However, efficiency introduces a subtle risk: the temptation to prioritise speed over intellectual engagement.

For academics, this is not a trivial concern.

If AI is used primarily to:

- Generate content quickly.
- Reduce effort.
- Bypass critical thinking.

It may lead to a gradual erosion of:

- Conceptual depth.
- Originality.
- Scholarly voice.

The challenge, therefore, is to use AI in a way that enhances thinking rather than replaces it. This requires deliberate choices, such as:

- Using AI to explore alternatives rather than settle on the first output.
- Engaging critically with generated content.
- Maintaining ownership of ideas and arguments.

In this sense, responsible use of AI is less about restriction and more about discipline.

8.5. Reclaiming the Academic Voice

A recurring concern among educators is that AI-generated content may lead to a loss of individual voice. This concern is valid, but it is not inevitable. The academic voice is shaped by experience, perspective, and disciplinary orientation. AI does not possess these; it generates text-based patterns, not lived intellectual engagement.

Therefore, rather than replacing the academic voice, AI should be used to:

- Support expression.
- Clarify ideas.
- Expand possibilities.

The final output, whether a lecture, assessment, or paper, should still reflect the lecturer's interpretation, the researcher's argument and the educator's intent.

In this way, AI becomes a supporting instrument, not the author.

8.6. Institutional and Disciplinary Considerations

It is also important to recognise that the integration of AI into academic practice does not occur in a vacuum. Different institutions and disciplines may have varying guidelines, different expectations regarding AI use and distinct epistemological traditions. For example:

- Quantitative disciplines may use AI differently from interpretative fields (as discussed in sections above).
- Professional programmes may emphasise applied use cases.
- Research-intensive institutions may prioritise originality and rigour.

As such, academics must navigate not only the capabilities of AI but also the norms and expectations of their context. As routines become more automated, the value of uniquely human capabilities becomes more visible.

In this evolving landscape, prompt engineering can be seen as part of a broader shift – from information delivery to intellectual design.

Academics are no longer transmitters of knowledge. They are:

- Designers of learning experiences.
- Curators of information.
- Facilitators of critical inquiry.

AI, when used thoughtfully, can support this transformation.

9. CONCLUSION

This chapter has examined how prompt engineering can be meaningfully integrated into core academic practices – ranging from research design and literature review to assessment and lecture design. Across these domains, a consistent insight emerges: the value of Gen AI does not lie in its ability to produce outputs quickly but in its capacity to extend and structure academic thinking when used deliberately. The cyclical model introduced in this chapter – define, design, generate, evaluate, and refine – provides a practical framework for this engagement. It emphasises that prompting is not a one-step interaction but an iterative process in which evaluation is embedded within design. This cycle makes academic expertise more visible, not less. Taken together, the discussions in this chapter suggest that prompt engineering, when used effectively, does not simplify academic work. Instead, it reconfigures it, making processes such as framing, evaluation, and refinement more explicit and more deliberate. In doing so, it offers an opportunity to strengthen – not dilute – the rigour of academic practice.

In the next chapter, we extend this discussion by examining how academics can engage with Gen AI using an ethical lens, ensuring that its use enhances credibility, integrity, and originality without compromising effectiveness.

REFERENCES

Alvesson, M., & Sandberg, J. (2011). Generating research questions through problematization. *Academy of Management Review*, *36*(2), 247–271.

Amershi, S., Weld, D., Vorvoreanu, M., Fourney, A., Nushi, B., Collisson, P., Suh, J., Iqbal, S., Bennett, P., Inkpen, K., Teevan, J., Kikin-Gil, R., & Horvitz, E. (2019). Guidelines for human–AI interaction. *Proceedings of the 2019 CHI Conference on Human Factors in Computing Systems*, 1–13. Association for Computing Machinery. https://doi.org/10.1145/3290605.3300233

Anderson, L. W., & Krathwohl, D. R. (2001). *A taxonomy for learning, teaching, and assessing*. Longman.

Bender, E. M., Gebru, T., McMillan-Major, A., & Shmitchell, S. (2021). On the dangers of stochastic parrots: Can language models be too big? *Proceedings of the 2021 ACM Conference on Fairness, Accountability, and Transparency*, 610–623. Association for Computing Machinery. https://doi.org/10.1145/3442188.3445922

Biggs, J. (1996). Enhancing teaching through constructive alignment. *Higher Education*, *32*(3), 347–364.

Biggs, J., & Tang, C. (2011). *Teaching for quality learning at university: What the student does*. McGraw-Hill.

Brown, T. B., Mann, B., Ryder, N., Subbiah, M., Kaplan, J., Dhariwal, P., Neelakantan, A., Shyam, P., Sastry, G., Askell, A., Agarwal, S., Herbert-Voss, A., Krueger, G., Henighan, T., Child, R., Ramesh, A., Ziegler, D. M., Wu, J., Winter, C., …, Amodei, D. (2020). Language models are few-shot learners. *Advances in Neural Information Processing Systems*, *33*, 1877–1901.

Boud, D., & Falchikov, N. (2007). *Rethinking assessment in higher education*. Routledge.

Corbin, J., & Strauss, A. (2015). *Basics of qualitative research*. Sage.

Creswell, J. W., & Creswell, J. D. (2018). *Research design: qualitative, quantitative, and mixed methods approaches*. Sage.

Dwivedi, Y. K., Kshetri, N., Hughes, L., Slade, E. L., Jeyaraj, A., Kar, A. K., Baabdullah, A. M., Koohang, A., Raghavan, V., Ahuja, M., Albanna, H., Albashrawi, M. A., Al-Busaidi, A. S., Balakrishnan, J., Barlette, Y., Basu, S., Bose, I., Brooks, L., Buhalis, D., …, Wright, R. (2023). So what if ChatGPT wrote it? Multidisciplinary perspectives on opportunities, challenges and implications of generative conversational AI for research, practice and policy. *International Journal of Information Management, 71*. https://doi.org/10.1016/j.ijinfomgt.2023.10264

Floridi, L. (2016). *The ethics of information*. Oxford University Press.

Gilson, A., Safranek, C., Huang, T., Socrates, V., Chi, L., Taylor, R., & Chartash, D. (2024). How does ChatGPT perform on the United States medical licensing examination (USMLE)? The implications of large language models for medical education and knowledge assessment. *JMIR Medical Education, 10*, e57594. https://doi.org/10.2196/57594.

Kasneci, E., Sessler, K., Kuchemann, S., Bannert, M., Dementieva, D., Fischer, F., Gasser, U., Groh, G., Günnemann, S., Hüllermeier, E., Krusche, S., Kutyniok, G., Michaeli, T., Nerdel, C., Pfeffer, J., Poquet, O., Sailer, M., Schmidt, A., Seidel, T., …, Kasneci, G. (2023). ChatGPT for good? On opportunities and challenges of large language models for education. *Learning and Individual Differences, 103*, 102274.

Laurillard, D. (2012). *Teaching as a design science*. Routledge. https://doi.org/10.4324/9780203125083

Nicol, D., & Macfarlane-Dick, D. (2006). Formative assessment and self-regulated learning: a model and seven principles of good feedback practice. *Studies in Higher Education, 31*(2), 199–218.

O'Neil, C. (2016). *Weapons of math destruction: How big data increases inequality and threatens democracy*. Crown.

Wei, J., Wang, X., Schuurmans, D., Bosma, M., Xia, F., Chi, E., Le, Q. V., & Zhou, D. (2022). Chain-of-thought prompting elicits reasoning in large language models. *Advances in Neural Information Processing Systems, 35*, 24824–24837.

Zawacki-Richter, O., Marín, V. I., Bond, M., & Gouverneur, F. (2019). Systematic review of research on artificial intelligence applications in higher education. *International Journal of Educational Technology in Higher Education, 16*(1), 1–27.

6

BALANCING INNOVATION AND ACADEMIC INTEGRITY

ABSTRACT

When discussing the use of generative artificial intelligence (Gen AI) in academia, it is important to address data privacy, intellectual property (IP), and legislative concerns, as these issues can impact the utilisation of artificial intelligence (AI) tools. Data privacy is a significant concern because Gen AI models require large amounts of data, which may include sensitive or personal information. Privacy breaches and data misuse may discourage academics from fully adopting these technologies. IP issues arise from how Gen AI models are trained and from the content they produce. These models often use copyrighted material without explicit permission, leading to disputes over ownership and the legality of AI-generated content. This ambiguity in IP rights can affect the adoption of AI in research, as academics may be unsure about the legal implications of using or publishing AI-generated work. Additionally, the legislative landscape surrounding Gen AI is still developing. Current laws may not fully address the challenges posed by AI, such as the attribution of generated content and the protection of proprietary data. This legal uncertainty can create challenges for academics who need clear guidelines to ensure compliance and protect their work. Addressing these concerns through comprehensive discussions and updated regulations are necessary for creating an environment where academics can use Gen AI effectively and ethically.

Keywords: Data privacy; bias in teaching and research; intellectual property concerns; ethical principles; human-in-the-loop; responsible use of AI

Chapter Goal: Show the ethical usage of Gen AI for academic purposes

1. INTRODUCTION

Using Gen AI in academia is an unfathomable transformation, amping up teaching experiences and research capabilities. However, academic leaders, teachers, and researchers are often sceptical about the responsible use of AI, data privacy, IP, and legislative concerns related to this innovation. These issues emphasise the need to balance them with the responsibility of the lecturers and researchers to uphold academic integrity. This chapter explores how to balance AI's technical attributes with the human values of lecturers and researchers, ensuring that AI serves as a research partner or colleague, assisting with teaching and research rather than stifling educators' independent thinking and originality.

2. RISKS ASSOCIATED WITH GEN AI IN TEACHING AND RESEARCH

Gen AI has the far-reaching potential to accelerate development across all sectors, from healthcare, marketing, and finance to education. However, several cases of judgemental errors by Gen AI across all sectors have been reported. Such cases highlight the risks and vulnerabilities associated with algorithmic errors and data mismanagement, compromising the integrity of AI systems. For example, some AI-based recruitment systems have resulted in significant gender and racial biases, some AI systems have evidently filtered out the best job applicants, and some AI chatbots have helped teen users plan violence (Dastin, 2018; Davis, 2024; Lytton, 2024; Polglase et al., 2026; Wilson & Caliskan, 2025). Further, incidents have been reported of ChatGPT hallucinating fictional cases in a legal brief (Neumeister, 2023). Thus, algorithmic errors and data mismanagement in AI systems risk disseminating false information or misinterpreting communications, generating socioeconomic disparities and societal bias, and leading to privacy breaches and may involve decisions made without human supervision, thereby posing ethical risks (Bostrom & Yudkowsky, 2018; Calo, 2017; Noble, 2018; O'Neil, 2017; Zarsky, 2016). Further, as the prominence of Gen AI in the education sector grows, it is crucial to understand the risks and vulnerabilities it poses, particularly for educators in teaching and research. The key AI-related concerns in teaching and research are:

2.1. Bias in Teaching and Research

Integrating AI technology into education has the potential to enhance personalised learning, improve course administration, and enable more effective research. However, AI systems have risks of bias, posing significant challenges in teaching and research, such as unfair treatment of students and skewed research outcomes. AI system bias in teaching and research manifests when the algorithms or data used to train these systems incorporate existing inequalities or stereotypical preferences, resulting in skewed teaching and research outcomes (Baker & Hawn, 2022).

2.1.1. Personalised Learning Systems

A typical AI system is trained on large amounts of data, which the model uses to learn and generate outputs. Lecturers can use AI solutions to create a personalised learning platform that recommends different learning paths for students with varying abilities. However, the developers may unknowingly train the model on biased data, leading the system to recommend learning paths for students based on biased assumptions, thereby reinforcing existing disparities by limiting educational opportunities for students from underrepresented groups (Holstein et al., 2019).

2.1.2. Automated Grading System

AI can be trained to evaluate student essays and assignments and automate grading, typically making the process much more efficient. However, there can be biases in these systems, as algorithms may unfairly favour certain writing styles or content over others based on the data they are trained on, resulting in rigid grading practices (Reich, 2020). For example, the AI grading system can give higher scores to students writing their essays in standard academic English and lower scores to students from diverse linguistic backgrounds (Reich, 2020).

2.1.3 Data Collection and Analysis

Impactful research often relies on large datasets for analysis. Biased datasets may yield skewed findings, leading to inaccurate conclusions and recommendations by lecturers and researchers. For example, a research study analysing student performance using AI systems may neglect a comprehensive list of factors influencing a specific student group if the data does not represent the entire student population (Barocas et al., 2023).

2.2. Data Privacy

Gen AI models require large datasets for training, which may include sensitive or personal information. This opens the door to privacy breaches and data misuse, raising significant concerns among lecturers and researchers about the ethical direction for protecting privacy and discouraging their full use of these AI technologies (Golda et al., 2024; Ng et al., 2025; Wu et al., 2024). The collection and processing of personal data by Gen AI models raise significant privacy concerns regarding data protection, user consent, and the rights of educators and researchers, as discussed below.

2.2.1. Memorise Training Data

Because a Gen AI model is trained on large datasets, it memorises excerpts of those datasets. This memorisation by Gen AI may later be 'recalled' in response to another user's prompt, posing risks for lecturers and researchers when analysing sensitive data (Hadad, 2023; Satvaty et al., 2024).

2.2.2. Lack of Data Control

If researchers input data into a commercial AI tool, such as the free version of ChatGPT, they tend to offer them a licence to use that data to train future models. This lack of data control results in a third-party data leak, violating Institutional Review Board (IRB) ethical approvals and data-sharing agreements (Alduais et al., 2025; Chauhan & Dutta, 2025; French, 2020).

2.2.3. De-identification Risks

Because AI excels at pattern matching, it is undoubtedly a great innovation for lecturers to assist with tasks such as assessment and grading and to provide immediate, meaningful student feedback (Future Nation Schools, 2023).

However, pattern matching can 're-identify' anonymous individuals by linking scattered data points, such as rare or specific pointers within a prompt or a dataset, posing de-identification risks for researchers and lecturers (Staufer et al., 2024).

2.3. IP Concerns

Gen AI models often use copyrighted material without explicit permission, leading to ownership disputes and legal challenges over AI-generated content. Because researchers follow the 'publish or perish' code, they worry that submitting their unpublished work or unique dataset to Gen AI may leak their original research ideas or generate them for another user before they can claim the due credit for their work (Mehta, 2025; Šarčević et al., 2024). They are concerned about the use of their copyrighted material in training AI models and about the ambiguities surrounding the legal implications of using or publishing AI-generated work. Thus, the complex and legally challenging IP concerns related to the fair use and ownership of AI-generated content may affect their use for research purposes (Afuwape, 2025; Rai, 2025).

2.4. Loss of Trust

For scientific research to be credible, it must be reproducible by other researchers. However, Gen AI is a black box with opaque training datasets, leading to a lack of verifiability of AI output and hindering reproducibility (Desai et al., 2025). This lack of transparency calls the trustworthiness of AI-based research into question (IAES, 2024). Further, Gen AI can create misleading or fraudulent research papers, raising concerns about the trustworthiness of AI-generated fake news and deepfake technologies (Folorunsho & Boamah, 2025; IAES, 2024). If AI-based research is not credible and trustworthy, the entire adoption and use of Gen AI models may decline, leading to a loss of trust.

To mitigate AI-related risks and vulnerabilities, it is critical to follow responsible AI practices that ensure AI models are transparent, unbiased, and respect human diversity and privacy (Radanliev et al., 2024). Thus, modelling *Responsible AI* that incorporates ethical principles into system design is key.

3. RESPONSIBLE AI IN EDUCATION: MITIGATING RISKS RELATED TO BIAS, PRIVACY, IP, AND TRUST

Responsible AI refers to the ethical and moral framework for the development, deployment, and use of AI systems, ensuring they are fair, transparent, and aligned with human values and societal norms (Jedličková, 2025; Radanliev et al., 2024). Responsible AI is key to mitigating the growing risks of AI use in educational contexts and to ensuring that AI is an ethical and effective tool for teaching and research. The following guidelines are critical for implementing responsible AI practices in the educational context, including transparent and unbiased AI systems that respect human privacy and diversity.

3.1. Incorporate Ethical Principles

Bias in Gen AI models poses significant risks to both teaching and research. It is paramount not only to have a clear understanding of the various biases in education but also to develop strategies to mitigate these risks and ensure that AI technologies are used responsibly and equitably. Bias in AI may arise from historical inequalities in the training data or from algorithms unintentionally biased towards a specific group (Mehrabi et al., 2021). Ethical principles are the cornerstone of responsible AI practices in the development and deployment of Gen AI systems to prevent bias and discrimination. In education, ethical AI models facilitate teaching if they are designed to:

3.1.1. Promote Fairness

Promote fairness by treating all students impartially and without prejudice, regardless of their background. Thus, AI models must be trained on diverse and representative datasets, minimising biases that could be unfair and unreasonable for certain groups (Mehrabi et al., 2021).

3.1.2. Ensure Accountability

Ensure developers and institutions are accountable for the outcomes of AI models. Regular audits and impact assessments must be conducted to check for any biases and errors and roll them back (Floridi et al., 2018).

3.1.3. Foster Inclusivity

Foster inclusivity so that AI tools are equally accessible to all students, including those with disabilities and those from minority groups and underrepresented communities. The AI models should be designed as effective teaching tools that cater to students with diverse needs and learning styles (Guspian et al., 2025; Salas-Pilco et al., 2022).

In summary, educational institutions must acknowledge the challenges of fairness, data privacy, and transparency and highlight the importance of responsible AI when designing and developing their Gen AI systems (Leong & Zhang, 2025; Memarian & Doleck, 2023). AI models are effective teaching tools if designed to promote fairness and inclusivity, ensuring that all students have equal learning opportunities. To mitigate bias and emphasise fairness, accountability, and transparency, educational institutions must adhere to ethical practices. Two key practices for identifying and mitigating bias are *conducting regular audits* of AI systems and *involving diverse stakeholders* in the design and evaluation processes (Floridi et al., 2018). *Regular audits and evaluations by diverse stakeholders*, such as lecturers, researchers, students, and AI experts, can help AI models identify and mitigate biases in teaching and research (Raji et al., 2020). By adopting these ethical principles, lecturers and researchers can nurture an AI-driven environment of learning and growth without supporting discrimination.

3.2. Data Quality

The data used to train the AI model in education must be accurate and reliable. Good data quality during training can help control several issues related to bias and discrimination in the generated output. On the other hand, AI models trained on incomplete or skewed data may exhibit poor data quality, leading to biased outcomes and erroneous predictions or recommendations (Žliobaitė, 2017). In the context of education, such biased outcomes may mislead lecturers in their assessment of student performance. To mitigate bias and improve data quality, the institutions should focus on:

3.2.1. Diverse Representative Datasets

Educational institutions should use diverse, representative datasets to train AI models, with algorithms that provide a wide range of experiences and perspectives (Gebru et al., 2021). The data diversity of the student population helps avoid skewed results. This involves collecting data from various demographic groups and ensuring it is comprehensive and up-to-date (Gebru et al., 2021).

3.2.2. Rigorous Data Collection and Validation Processes

Rigorous data collection and validation processes ensure that the data is thoroughly checked for errors, inconsistencies, and missing values (Aldoseri et al., 2023). The dataset representing a diverse student population for training AI models is free of errors and inconsistencies, thereby maintaining the integrity of the data used. Further, validated datasets vetted by experts can enhance the credibility and reliability of AI systems.

Thus, institutions emphasise the use of high-quality data when training their AI models, thereby reducing the risk of bias and discrimination and ensuring the reliability of AI-driven outputs (Gebru et al., 2021).

3.3. Data Transparency

Data transparency is significant for building trust in AI systems for teaching and research. Transparency refers to providing clear information about the development, functionality, and decision-making processes adopted by AI models (Ananny & Crawford, 2018). Transparency in the context of education involves the following:

3.3.1. Open Communication

Open communication by the institutions about the data sources, algorithms, and decision-making processes behind AI models. This enhances transparency and allows lecturers and researchers to understand the limitations of AI outcomes and maximise its advantages (Ananny & Crawford, 2018).

3.3.2. Documentation and Institutional Access

Documentation and institutional access to AI models help lecturers and researchers probe AI outcomes and hold developers liable for errors and inconsistencies (Nguyen & Nguyen, 2025).

3.3.3. Engaging Students, Teachers, and Researchers

Engaging students, teachers, and researchers in the design and evaluation of AI models to enhance transparency and ensure that the AI tool is effective in serving the teaching and research needs of its users (Felzmann et al., 2020).

In other words, transparent and explainable AI models can help lecturers and researchers interpret the model, understand the decision-making process, identify biases, and eventually correct them (Lipton, 2018). In an educational context, transparent AI systems refer to providing educators, lecturers, and researchers with access to information about the data sources, algorithms, and decision-making processes used in Gen AI models. It enables teachers and researchers to understand the AI-generated outputs and their limitations, thus reducing the risk of bias and discrimination. Educational institutions should focus on open communication, recording, and documentation for algorithmic decision-making, enabling educational users to examine and inspect AI models and hold developers accountable (Diakopoulos, 2016). By promoting data transparency in AI models, educational institutions may enhance trust in Gen AI technologies and ensure their responsible use.

3.4. Mitigating Privacy

To address the privacy concerns associated with training Gen AI not to disclose academic data and information, academic institutions must implement robust data governance frameworks to ensure compliance with privacy regulations such as the General Data Protection Regulation (GDPR) (Voigt & Von dem Bussche, 2017). Such institutions often employ specific *Privacy-Enhancing Technologies (PETs)* as critical technical components of data governance frameworks to balance the accuracy of the results with privacy requirements (Jansen et al., 2025). Some of these PETs include:

3.4.1. Differential Privacy (DP)

DP injects carefully calibrated random noise into the data during training, ensuring that the output is almost identical even with a single datapoint, thus allowing for accurate aggregate analysis (Dwork & Roth, 2014). Though it limits the amount of information or data leaked or 'memorised' by Gen AI, it often results in high noise and lower accuracy of results in Gen AI (Alzoubi & Mishra, 2025). DP facilitates the teaching process by protecting student data while enabling useful AI-driven insights.

3.4.2. Federated Learning (FL)

FL is a decentralised mechanism that ensures raw data remains at its original location, which may be the university server (Shukla, 2024). This provides for training AI models across multiple decentralised devices without sharing raw data (McMahan et al., 2017). Thus, universities train a local model and send only encrypted AI gradients to a central server to improve the global model. Because sensitive information and student data remain on local devices, they are better controlled, privacy is enhanced, and the risk of data breaches is reduced, thus mitigating privacy concerns during teaching and research.

3.4.3. Generating Synthetic Data

Generating synthetic data that mimics the statistical properties of real data without exposing any personal identifiers or other sensitive information (Patki et al., 2016). Such an approach enables 'data desensitisation' and allows researchers to share datasets for broader academic use while preserving participants' privacy (Wang et al., 2025). Thus, synthetic data can be used to train AI models for better teaching experiences while preserving student privacy.

3.4.4. Self-hosted Local Large Language Models (LLMs)

Self-hosted local LLMs, rather than relying on commercial cloud-based AI, are the technique adopted by many academic institutions to have maximum control. These models run on university-owned hardware or private servers using tools such as Ollama or LM Studio, creating an 'air-gapped' environment that keeps the data within the institution, thereby satisfying IRB requirements (Josa & Bleda-Bejar, 2024). The local deployment of LLMs on institutional servers ensures institutional control over data, thereby enhancing privacy and security for better teaching and research.

3.4.5. Advanced Cryptography

Advanced cryptography, such as homomorphic encryption, allows AI to perform computations on encrypted data at all times and can only be read by the original data owner (Feretzakis et al., 2024). Another cryptographic technique is secure multi-party computation, which allows multiple parties to jointly compute an output without any single party gaining access to the others' private inputs (Feretzakis et al., 2024). Such techniques enable privacy-preserving AI analysis by allowing computations over encrypted data (Gentry, 2009). To address privacy concerns for lecturers and researchers, academic institutions mostly balance the privacy strength of the technique with computational cost, such as the extra processing power and time required.

Although PETs are not legal solutions, they are innovative and practical actions to enable 'privacy by design and default' (GDPR Article 25) (OneTrust, 2026). For example, data sharing is undeniably the backbone of academic learning and research, but PETs such as DP help to minimise data and information processed by adding 'noise' or aggregating data. Another such example is FL, which allows academic institutions to keep their raw data on their local servers while still enabling collaboration. At the same time, Gen AI models are trained on decentralised data across multiple institutions (OneTrust, 2026). Despite PETs' ability to support academic data governance and compliance, if not implemented correctly, they can be vulnerable to attack and require consistent monitoring (Harmeling, 2026). Often, this requires a broader data governance framework that combines legal, social, and policy controls to be truly effective for teaching and research.

Academic institutions must strive to establish a clear legal and ethical framework for understanding the fair use of AI-generated content and copyrighted data in AI model training and for clarifying ownership of outputs (Benson, 2025). Fair use by AI refers to the limited use of copyrighted material without permission for education and research. It is driven by the fact that even human researchers rely on multiple sources to generate new insights (Sourcely, 2025). However, training AI models on vast amounts of data is often criticised for generating content that exceeds fair use boundaries; therefore, consent and compliance become critical in teaching and research.

3.5. Consent and Compliance

Consent and compliance are significant in mitigating privacy concerns in AI-driven teaching and research practices. The collection and use of data for teaching and research must comply with legal and ethical standards, such as the GDPR in Europe or the Family Educational Rights and Privacy Act (FERPA) in the United States (Chauhan & Dutta, 2025; Parks, 2017). These regulations require that students and their guardians provide informed consent before their data can be collected and used.

Informed consent in AI education enables students and guardians to remain fully informed about how their data will be used for teaching and research and to opt out if they wish (Huang, 2023). Transparency regarding informed consent ensures that institutions adopt ethical data practices in AI-driven teaching and research practices, thereby building trust in them (Mienye & Swart, 2025). Educational institutions must adhere to these regulations by implementing clear consent mechanisms that prevent misunderstandings among students about how their data will be used and that allow them to opt out if they wish. Compliance with privacy regulations in educational institutions has a twofold advantage: protecting student data and building trust in

AI systems by showcasing a commitment to ethical data practices (Huang, 2023; Peña et al., 2024).

3.6. Monitor and Improve

Continuous monitoring and improvement of AI models are critical to maintain their effectiveness and tackle potential biases. In education, AI models should be regularly evaluated to ensure their accuracy and fairness over time (Binns, 2018; Oyeniran et al., 2022). To monitor and improve such AI systems, educational institutions should continually track their performance, identify variances in generated outputs, and fine-tune their algorithms or data sources accordingly. To ensure continuous monitoring and improvement, educational institutions must establish clear feedback loops that enable lecturers and researchers to raise issues or concerns related to the use of Gen AI and its outputs. This feedback enables ongoing improvement and helps prevent the perpetuation of any system bias (Veale & Binns, 2017). Through continued monitoring and improvement, lecturers and researchers would feel confident that Gen AI is beneficial and equitable for all users.

3.7. Human-in-the-Loop

The human-in-the-loop approach underscores the importance of human oversight in AI systems, especially in education (Kumar et al., 2024). Although AI can provide useful insights and automate many critical tasks, human judgement is indispensable for critically analysing, interpreting, and applying AI-driven insights meaningfully (Adamakis & Rachiotis, 2025). In educational contexts, lecturers and researchers should:

Actively participate in deploying and using Gen AI, ensuring it complements rather than replaces human expertise.

Ethically evaluate and contextualise the knowledge that may be lacking in AI models. This approach also allows for incorporating ethical considerations and contextual knowledge that AI systems may lack (Holstein et al., 2019).

By balancing AI capabilities with human judgement and maintaining a human-in-the-loop approach to address human inaccuracies and oversight, educational institutions can reduce risks associated with over-reliance on AI and prevent the loss of trust in AI-generated content. By maintaining this human-in-the-loop approach, lecturers and researchers stay insulated against its limitations while fully exploiting its potential.

3.8. Ownership of AI-generated Content and IP Rights Issue

The key question regarding the use of AI-generated content for teaching and research remains: *who owns it?* This is because the way AI models are trained and the content they produce often exceed fair use boundaries for copyrighted material without explicit permission (Murray, 2023; Sobel, 2017). This ambiguity regarding the ownership and legality of AI-generated content may adversely affect the use of AI in research, as lecturers and researchers may be unsure about the legal implications of using or publishing such work. Although traditional IP laws strictly protect human authorship, it is not easy to extend them to AI-generated works (Gaffar & Albarashdi, 2025; Gaidartzi & Stamatoudi, 2025). The fear of infringing on IP rights due to a lack of clear guidelines may discourage lecturers and researchers from using Gen AI.

Academic institutions and policymakers must develop *clear guidelines and frameworks* for the use of AI-generated content. These guidelines should ensure the legal and ethical use of AI tools by addressing concerns about IP rights for AI-generated content and the use of copyrighted materials in training datasets and by setting clear policies for academic institutions on proper licencing agreements and attribution requirements (Zakir et al., 2024). Furthermore, *open-access initiatives* for AI tools and datasets can facilitate knowledge and resource sharing, support collaborative research, and encourage the responsible use of AI technologies for teaching and research (Dergaa & Saad, 2023).

4. GUIDELINES ON USING GEN AI AS AN ACADEMIC COLLABORATOR

Incidents of AI-generated biases and fabricated cases in ChatGPT-generated legal briefs clearly highlight the need to balance and control this powerful and consequential AI technology through responsible use for teaching and research. Although Gen AI, such as LLMs, has opened novel avenues for collaboration in academia, most journals and universities require human authorship per the degree of human creative control in AI-assisted work and do not permit listing an AI tool as a co-author (Kotsis, 2025; Members' Research Service, 2025; Moffatt & Hall, 2025). Despite its ability to assist with content generation and data analysis and to provide deep insights, thus serving as a valuable AI collaborator for human researchers and educators, its use necessitates careful consideration of ethical, practical, and methodological guidelines to ensure that it is integrated effectively and responsibly into academic work, producing unbiased, accurate, and contextual information. The lecturers and researchers should keep the following points in mind:

4.1. Aware of Gen AI Capabilities and Acknowledge Its Limitations

Before using Gen AI as an academic collaborator for educational tasks such as drafting text, summarising literature, and generating hypotheses, lecturers and researchers should understand its capabilities and limitations. They should appreciate the functionalities of the AI tool, such as the tasks it can perform and the quality of outputs it typically generates (Khalifa & Albadawy, 2024). Further, beyond capability awareness, they should understand and acknowledge the limitations of AI tools, such as their over-reliance on training data, potential inaccuracies and biases, and the limitations of Gen AI to comprehend the nuances of an academic setting. Such understanding helps them evaluate AI-generated content effectively.

4.2. Ensure Ethical Use

Lecturers and researchers should ensure that while using Gen AI as an academic collaborator, they uphold academic integrity and ethical standards. Because ethical considerations while using Gen AI in academia are predominant, the academic community should adopt the following practices when using it for teaching or research.

Ensure transparency by acknowledging AI inputs and disclosing the use of Gen AI in publications, presentations, and other academic work (Tang et al., 2024). Next, they should *avoid plagiarism* by ensuring that the AI-generated content is original and properly attributed with citations and references (Alawad et al., 2025; Hutson, 2024). Although it's a good idea to use AI tools for generating new ideas and creating drafts, human intervention by critically reviewing and refining the content is important to maintain academic integrity (Khalifa & Albadawy, 2024). Finally, *mitigate biases* by staying vigilant about potential inaccuracies and inconsistencies in AI-generated content. It is important to regularly review AI-generated output for biases in language and content and make appropriate adjustments to ensure fairness and inclusivity (Afreen et al., 2025).

4.3. Integrate AI with Human Skills

Lecturers and researchers should integrate the potential of Gen AI with human capabilities to enable effective collaboration between humans and AI, resulting in AI-driven academic and research outcomes that complement rather than replace human skills. Because effective collaboration between AI and humans is the key, the academic community should adopt the following practices:

Stay vigilant with AI-generated content by reviewing, editing, and contextualising outputs to ensure alignment with academic requirements and objectives (Mohamed et al., 2024). Next, *use AI collaboratively* in research or teaching that involves generating initial drafts or conducting data analysis, followed by human skill to refine and interpret the idea (Fan & Zhong, 2022). Finally, *develop AI-related skills*, such as AI literacy and critical thinking, to effectively use and evaluate AI tools and to critically assess AI-generated content (Annapureddy et al., 2025; Tadimalla & Maher, 2025).

4.4. Consider Data Privacy and Security

Lecturers and researchers should consider data privacy and security when using AI to handle sensitive academic and student data by doing the following:

Protect data by ensuring its use complies with relevant data protection regulations, such as anonymising data and securing required permissions (Huang, 2023). Further, they should *use secure, reputable AI platforms* that prioritise data privacy and security (Jose, 2024).

4.5. Evaluate AI-generated Outputs

Lecturers and researchers should critically evaluate the AI-generated output to maintain the quality and relevance of their academic work by adopting the following practices:

Assess and verify the quality of AI-generated content, such as educational resources for university teaching and learning, by checking its accuracy and relevance to the academic context (Huang et al., 2025). Further, they should *adopt feedback mechanisms* and use iterative processes to help AI developers refine AI-generated content (Talaver & Vakaliuk, 2024).

4.6. Encourage Responsible Use

Lecturers and researchers should be encouraged to use Gen AI responsibly for innovation and idea generation to enhance teaching and research by adopting the following practices:

Apply Gen AI innovatively to enhance learning and research, such as using personalised learning experiences or novel research methods (Laak & Aru, 2025). Further, they should *pursue collaborative research projects* to explore the potential and novel applications of Gen AI for academics and to enhance AI's role in education and research (Alasadi & Baiz, 2023).

In conclusion, Gen AI has far-reaching potential as an academic collaborator with educators, offering new dimensions and a range of scenarios for research and education. By following the suggested guidelines, educators can responsibly and effectively harness AI's potential, ensuring it augments human skills, works well with them, and upholds ethical standards. These guidelines serve as a blueprint for educators and researchers, helping them leverage the far-reaching potential of Gen AI and harness its benefits while remaining cognisant of its limitations.

5. CONCLUSION

Integrating AI into education offers state-of-the-art and unprecedented possibilities but poses significant ethical challenges. As Gen AI becomes an indispensable tool in teaching and research, educators, researchers, and institutions must adopt responsible AI practices to use it effectively. In this chapter, we presented various dimensions of responsible AI, emphasising the significance of ethical principles, data quality, transparency, privacy, consent, compliance, continuous monitoring, and human intervention. These foundational features collectively ensure that Gen AI is developed and deployed to promote fairness, inclusivity, and accountability while preventing bias and discrimination.

Privacy-enhancing techniques such as DP, FL, and advanced cryptography are key to safeguarding sensitive student data. At the same time, clear guidelines on IP rights and open-access initiatives present another critical dimension of AI-generated content. By understanding and respecting these ethical considerations, educational institutions can build trust in Gen AI and use this tool for innovation and collaboration.

REFERENCES

Adamakis, M., & Rachiotis, T. (2025). Artificial intelligence in higher education: A state-of-the-art overview of pedagogical integrity, artificial intelligence literacy, and policy integration. *Encyclopedia*, *5*(4), 180.

Afreen, J., Mohaghegh, M., & Doborjeh, M. (2025). Systematic literature review on bias mitigation in generative AI. *AI and Ethics*, *5*(5), 4789–4841.

Afuwape, K. (2025). Ethical implications of using artificial intelligence in intellectual property creation: Authorship, ownership and responsibility issues. *Journal of Digital Technologies and Law*, *3*(4), 677–704.

Alasadi, E. A., & Baiz, C. R. (2023). Generative AI in education and research: Opportunities, concerns, and solutions. *Journal of Chemical Education*, *100*(8), 2965–2971.

Alawad, E. A., Ayadi, H. H., & Alhinai, A. A. (2025). Guarding integrity: A case study on tackling AI generated content and plagiarism in academic writing. *Theory and Practice in Language Studies*, *15*(6), 1730–1742.

Aldoseri, A., Al-Khalifa, K. N., & Hamouda, A. M. (2023). Re-thinking data strategy and integration for artificial intelligence: Concepts, opportunities, and challenges. *Applied Sciences*, *13*(12), 7082.

Alduais, A., Qadhi, S., Chaaban, Y., & Khraisheh, M. (2025). Utilising generative AI responsibly and ethically for research purposes in higher education: A policy analysis. *Serials Review*, *51*(3–4), 120–170.

Alzoubi, Y. I., & Mishra, A. (2025). Differential privacy and artificial intelligence: Potentials, challenges, and future avenues. *EURASIP Journal on Information Security*, *2025*(1), 18.

Ananny, M., & Crawford, K. (2018). Seeing without knowing: Limitations of the transparency ideal and its application to algorithmic accountability. *New Media & Society*, *20*(3), 973–989.

Annapureddy, R., Fornaroli, A., & Gatica-Perez, D. (2025). Generative AI literacy: Twelve defining competencies. *Digital Government: Research and Practice*, *6*(1), 1–21.

Baker, R. S., & Hawn, A. (2022). Algorithmic bias in education. *International Journal of Artificial Intelligence in Education*, *32*(4), 1052–1092.

Barocas, S., Hardt, M., & Narayanan, A. (2023). *Fairness and machine learning: Limitations and opportunities*. MIT Press.

Benson, S. (2025, May 27). *Copyright and generative AI training: Infringment or fair use?* University of Illinois Ubraba Champaign. Retrieved March 30, from https://www.library.illinois.edu/scp/podcast/copyright-and-generative-ai-training-infringment-or-fair-use/#:~:text=The%20other%20thing%20I%20want,them%20in%20the%20existing%20markets

Binns, R. (2018). Fairness in machine learning: Lessons from political philosophy. In *Proceedings of the 2018 Conference on Fairness, Accountability and Transparency* (Vol. 81, pp. 149–159). Proceedings of Machine Learning Research.

Bostrom, N., & Yudkowsky, E. (Eds.). (2018). The ethics of artificial intelligence. In *Artificial intelligence safety and security* (pp. 57–69). Chapman and Hall/CRC.

Calo, R. (2017). Artificial intelligence policy: A primer and roadmap. *UC Davis Law Review*, *51*, 399.

Chauhan, S., & Dutta, A. (2025). Artificial intelligence in student privacy and data security. *International Journal of Advanced Research in Computer Science*, *16*(3). https://doi.org/10.26483/ijarcs.v16i3.7261

Dastin, J. (2018, October 11). *Insight – Amazon scraps secret AI recruiting tool that showed bias against women*. Reuters. Retrieved March 31, from https://www.reuters.com/article/world/insight-amazon-scraps-secret-ai-recruiting-tool-that-showed-bias-against-women-idUSKCN1MK0AG/#:~:text=That%20is%20because%20Amazon's%20computer,prove%20discriminatory%2C%20the%20people%20said

Davis, N. (2024, March 11). *UK report reveals bias within medical tools and devices*. Retrieved March 31, from https://www.theguardian.com/society/2024/mar/11/medical-tools-devices-healthcare-bias-uk

Dergaa, I., & Saad, H. B. (2023). Artificial intelligence and promoting open access in academic publishing. *La Tunisie Medicale*, *101*(6), 533.

Desai, A., Abdelhamid, M., & Padalkar, N. R. (2025). What is reproducibility in artificial intelligence and machine learning research? *AI Magazine*, *46*(2), e70004.

Diakopoulos, N. (2016). Accountability in algorithmic decision making. *Communications of the ACM*, *59*(2), 56–62.

Dorca Josa, A., & Bleda-Bejar, M. (2024). Local LLMs: Safeguarding data privacy in the age of generative AI: A case study at the University of Andorra. In *ICERI2024 Proceedings* (pp. 7879–7888). IATED Academy. https://doi.org/10.21125/iceri.2024.1931

Dwork, C., & Roth, A. (2014). The algorithmic foundations of differential privacy. *Foundations and Trends® in Theoretical Computer Science*, *9*(3–4), 211–487.

Fan, X., & Zhong, X. (2022). Artificial intelligence-based creative thinking skill analysis model using human–computer interaction in art design teaching. *Computers and Electrical Engineering*, *100*, 107957.

Felzmann, H., Fosch-Villaronga, E., Lutz, C., & Tamò-Larrieux, A. (2020). Towards transparency by design for artificial intelligence. *Science and Engineering Ethics*, *26*(6), 3333–3361.

Feretzakis, G., Papaspyridis, K., Gkoulalas-Divanis, A., & Verykios, V. S. (2024). Privacy-preserving techniques in generative AI and large language models: A narrative review. *Information*, *15*(11), 697.

Floridi, L., Cowls, J., Beltrametti, M., Chatila, R., Chazerand, P., Dignum, V., Luetge, C., Madelin, R., Pagallo, U., Rossi, F., Schafer, B., Valcke, P., & Vayena, E. (2018). AI4People—An ethical framework for a good AI society: Opportunities, risks, principles, and recommendations. *Minds and machines*, *28*(4), 689–707.

Folorunsho, F., & Boamah, B. F. (2025). Deepfake technology and its impact: Ethical considerations, societal disruptions, and security threats in AI-generated media. *International Journal of Information Technology and Management Information Systems*, *16*(1), 1060–1080.

French, C. (2020, Sep 10). *Human + machine*. Medium. Retrieved March 25, from https://medium.com/swlh/human-machine-3b9c535bc6c8

Future Nation Schools. (2023, June 7). *AI's impact on education: Why parents and teachers need to leverage AI for our children's sake*. Future Nation Schools. https://futurenationschools.com/ais-impact-on-education-why-parents-and-teachers-need-to-leverage-ai-for-our-childrens-sake/

Gaffar, H., & Albarashdi, S. (2025). Copyright protection for AI-generated works: Exploring originality and ownership in a digital landscape. *Asian Journal of International Law*, *15*(1), 23–46.

Gaidartzi, A., & Stamatoudi, I. (2025). Authorship and ownership issues raised by AI-generated works: A comparative analysis. *Laws*, *14*(4), 57.

Gebru, T., Morgenstern, J., Vecchione, B., Vaughan, J. W., Wallach, H., Daumé, H., & Crawford, K. (2021). Datasheets for datasets. *Communications of the ACM*, *64*(12), 86–92.

Gentry, C. (2009). Fully homomorphic encryption using ideal lattices. In *Proceedings of the 41st Annual ACM Symposium on Theory of Computing* (pp. 169–178). Association for Computing Machinery.

Golda, A., Mekonen, K., Pandey, A., Singh, A., Hassija, V., Chamola, V., & Sikdar, B. (2024). Privacy and security concerns in generative AI: A comprehensive survey. *IEEE Access*, *12*, 48126–48144.

Guspian, I., Lin, C.-C., YuQing Huang, A., & Yang, S. J. (2025). Challenges, practices, and research issues of diversity and inclusion in artificial intelligence for sustainable education. *International Journal on Advanced Science, Engineering & Information Technology*, *15*(5), 1387–1394.

Hadad, U. (2023, July 11). It's time for some machine UNlearning. Privya. Retrieved March 25, from https://privya.ai/blog/its-time-for-some-machine-unlearning/#:~:text=When%20ML%20(%20machine%20learning%20(ML%20),data%20points%2C%20taken%20from%20across%20the%20internet

Harmeling, T. (2026, March 25). *The value of privacy-enhancing technologies for businesses in 2026*. UserCentrics. Retrieved March 30, from https://usercentrics.com/guides/data-privacy/privacy-enhancing-technologies-value/#:~:text=Privacy%2Denhancing%20technologies%20(PETs)%20help%20businesses%20comply%20with%20the,marketing%20compliance%20requirements%20grow%20stricter

Holstein, K., Wortman Vaughan, J., Daumé III, H., Dudík, M., & Wallach, H. (2019). Improving fairness in machine learning systems: What do industry practitioners need? *Proceedings of the 2019 CHI Conference on Human Factors in Computing Systems*, 1–16. Association for Computing Machinery.

Huang, L. (2023). Ethics of artificial intelligence in education: Student privacy and data protection. *Science Insights Education Frontiers*, *16*(2), 2577–2587.

Huang, Q., Lv, C., Lu, L., & Tu, S. (2025). Evaluating the quality of AI-generated digital educational resources for university teaching and learning. *Systems*, *13*(3), 174.

Hutson, J. (2024). Rethinking plagiarism in the era of generative AI. *Journal of Intelligent Communication*, *3*(2), 20–31.

IAES. (2024, July 3). *Using AI for research, is it allowed?* Retrieved March 25, from https://www.iaesjournal.com/leveraging-artificial-intelligence-to-transform-modern-research-risks-and-ethical-considerations/#:~:text=Reproducibility%20is%20also%20a%20key%20issue.%20For,of%20many%20AI%20systems%20can%20hinder%20reproducibility

Jansen, R., Buckley, D., Jug, M., & Yao, K. (2025). How privacy enhancing technologies can advance responsible data sharing. *Statistical Journal of the IAOS*, *41*(3), 802–807.

Jedličková, A. (2025). Ethical approaches in designing autonomous and intelligent systems: A comprehensive survey towards responsible development. *AI & Society*, *40*(4), 2703–2716.

Jose, D. (2024). Data privacy and security concerns in AI-integrated educational platforms. *Recent Trends in Management and Commerce*, *5*(2), 87–91.

Khalifa, M., & Albadawy, M. (2024). Using artificial intelligence in academic writing and research: An essential productivity tool. *Computer Methods and Programs in Biomedicine Update*, *5*, 100145.

Kotsis, K. T. (2025). Redefining scientific authorship in the age of AI: Challenges for editors and institutions. *European Journal of Innovative Studies and Sustainability*, *1*(5), 23–33.

Kumar, S., Datta, S., Singh, V., Datta, D., Singh, S. K., & Sharma, R. (2024). Applications, challenges, and future directions of human-in-the-loop learning. *IEEE Access*, *12*, 75735–75760.

Laak, K.-J., & Aru, J. (2025). AI and personalised learning. *Educational Technology & Society*, *28*(4), 133–150.

Leong, W., & Zhang, J. (2025). Ethical design of AI for education and learning systems. *ASM Science Journal*, *20*(1), 1–9.

Lipton, Z. C. (2018). The mythos of model interpretability: In machine learning, the concept of interpretability is both important and slippery. *Queue*, *16*(3), 31–57.

Lytton, C. (2024, February 16). *AI hiring tools may be filtering out the best job applicants*. BBC. Retrieved March 30, from https://www.bbc.com/worklife/article/20240214-ai-recruiting-hiring-software-bias-discrimination

McMahan, B., Moore, E., Ramage, D., Hampson, S., & Agüera y Arcas, B. (2017). Communication-efficient learning of deep networks from decentralized data. In A. Singh & J. Zhu (Eds.), *Proceedings of the 20th International Conference on Artificial Intelligence and Statistics* (Vol. 54, pp. 1273–1282). Proceedings of Machine Learning Research. https://proceedings.mlr.press/v54/mcmahan17a.html

Mehrabi, N., Morstatter, F., Saxena, N., Lerman, K., & Galstyan, A. (2021). A survey on bias and fairness in machine learning. *ACM Computing Surveys (CSUR)*, *54*(6), 1–35.

Mehta, R. (2025, March 17). *Shadow AI & data leakage: How to secure generative AI at work*. Versa. Retrieved March 25, from https://versa-networks.com/blog/shadow-ai-data-leakage-how-to-secure-generative-ai-at-work/#:~:text=One%20of%20the%20most%20pressing%20risks%20is,it%20could%20potentially%20become%20accessible%20to%20others

Memarian, B., & Doleck, T. (2023). Fairness, accountability, transparency, and ethics (FATE) in artificial intelligence (AI) and higher education: A systematic review. *Computers and Education: Artificial Intelligence*, *5*, 100152.

Members' Research Service. (2025, April 28). *AI and copyright: The training of general-purpose AI*. European Parliament. Retrieved March 30, from https://epthinktank.eu/2025/04/28/ai-and-copyright-the-training-of-general%E2%80%91purpose-ai/#:~:text=To%20train%20their%20models%2C%20general,copyrighted%20materials%20for%20GPAI%20training

Mienye, I. D., & Swart, T. G. (2025). ChatGPT in education: A review of ethical challenges and approaches to enhancing transparency and privacy. *Procedia Computer Science*, *254*, 181–190.

Moffatt, B., & Hall, A. (2025). Is AI my co-author? The ethics of using artificial intelligence in scientific publishing. *Accountability in Research*, *32*(8), 1313–1329.

Mohamed, Y. A., Mohamed, A. H. H., Khanan, A., Bashir, M., Adiel, M. A., & Elsadig, M. A. (2024). Navigating the ethical terrain of AI-generated text tools: A review. *IEEE Access*, *12*, 197061–197120.

Murray, M. D. (2023). Generative AI art: Copyright infringement and fair use. *SMU Science & Technology Law Review*, *26*, 259.

Neumeister, L. (2023, June 9). *Lawyers blame ChatGPT for tricking them into citing bogus past cases in court. Los Angeles Times*. https://www.latimes.com/world-nation/story/2023-06-09/chatgpt-lawyers-cite-bogus-case-law

Ng, B. Y., Li, J., Tong, X., Ye, K., Yenne, G., Chandrasekaran, V., & Li, J. (2025). Analysing security and privacy challenges in generative AI usage guidelines for higher education. *arXiv preprint arXiv:2506.20463*.

Nguyen, P. B. T., & Nguyen, T. N. P. (2025). Ethical and responsible AI in educational use of ChatGPT. TPM–Testing, Psychometrics, Methodology in *Applied Psychology*, *32*(S7), 1322–1335.

Noble, S. U. (2018). Algorithms of oppression: How search engines reinforce racism. In *Algorithms of oppression*. New York University Press.

O'neil, C. (2017). *Weapons of math destruction: How big data increases inequality and threatens democracy*. Crown.

OneTrust. (2026). *Privacy-enhancing technologies (PETs)*. Retrieved March 30 from https://www.onetrust.com/glossary/privacy-enhancing-technologies-pets/#:~:text=enhancing%20technologies%20(PETs)-,What%20are%20privacy%2Denhancing%20technologies%20(PETs)?,by%2Ddesign%20principles%20at%20scale

Oyeniran, C., Adewusi, A. O., Adeleke, A. G., Akwawa, L. A., & Azubuko, C. F. (2022). Ethical AI: Addressing bias in machine learning models and software applications. *Computer Science & IT Research Journal*, *3*(3), 115–126.

Parks, C. (2017). Beyond compliance: Students and FERPA in the age of big data. *Journal of Intellectual Freedom and Privacy*, 2(2), 23.

Patki, N., Wedge, R., & Veeramachaneni, K. (2016). The synthetic data vault. In *2016 IEEE International Conference on Data Science and Advanced Analytics (DSAA)* (pp. 399–410). IEEE.

Peña, J. M., Moreno, O. B., Herrera, Á. L. O., & Moreno, T. E. B. (2024). Balancing privacy and ethics in the use of artificial intelligence in education. *Sapiens International Multidisciplinary Journal*, *1*(3), 148–170.

Polglase, K., Goodwin, A., & Gordon, A. (2026, March 11). 'Happy (and safe) shooting!' AI chatbots helped teen users plan violence in hundreds of tests. CNN. Retrieved March 31 from https://edition.cnn.com/2026/03/11/americas/ai-chatbots-help-teen-test-users-plan-violence-tests-intl-invs

Radanliev, P., Santos, O., Brandon-Jones, A., & Joinson, A. (2024). Ethics and responsible AI deployment. *Frontiers in Artificial Intelligence*, *7*, 1377011.

Rai, P. (2025). Generative AI in academia: Navigating copyright and intellectual property challenges. *Indian Journal of Educational Technology*, 7(II), 61–72.

Raji, I. D., Gebru, T., Mitchell, M., Buolamwini, J., Lee, J., & Denton, R. (2020). Saving face: Investigating the ethical concerns of facial recognition auditing. In *Proceedings of the AAAI/ACM Conference on AI, Ethics, and Society* (pp. 145–151). Association for Computing Machinery. https://doi.org/10.1145/3375627.3375820

Reich, J. (2020). *Failure to disrupt: Why technology alone can't transform education*. Harvard University Press.

Salas-Pilco, S. Z., Xiao, K., & Oshima, J. (2022). Artificial intelligence and new technologies in inclusive education for minority students: A systematic review. *Sustainability*, *14*(20), 13572.

Šarčević, T., Karlowicz, A., Mayer, R., Baeza-Yates, R., & Rauber, A. (2024). U can't Gen this? A survey of intellectual property protection methods for data in generative AI. arXiv preprint arXiv:2406.15386.

Satvaty, A., Verberne, S., & Turkmen, F. (2024). Undesirable memorisation in large language models: A survey. arXiv preprint arXiv:2410.02650.

Shukla, P. (2024, October 4). *Federated learning: Revolutionizing AI with privacy protection*. Medium. Retrieved March 25 from https://medium.com/accredian/federated-learning-revolutionizing-ai-with-privacy-protection-fc2e15c8e01d

Sobel, B. L. (2017). Artificial intelligence's fair use crisis. *The Columbia Journal of Law & The Arts*, *41*, 45.

Sourcely. (2025, June 4). *Fair use vs. copyright in AI searches*. Retrieved March 30, from https://www.sourcely.net/resources/fair-use-vs-copyright-in-ai-searches

Staufer, D., Pallas, F., & Berendt, B. (2024). *Silencing the risk, not the whistle: A semi-automated text sanitisation tool for mitigating the risk of Whistleblower re-identification* [Conference paper]. In Proceedings of the 2024 ACM conference on fairness, accountability, and transparency (13 pp). ACM.

Tadimalla, S. Y., & Maher, M. L. (2025). AI literacy as a core component of AI education. *AI magazine*, *46*(2), e70007.

Talaver, O. V., & Vakaliuk, T. A. (2024). *A model for improving the accuracy of educational content created by generative AI*. AREdu.

Tang, A., Li, K. K., Kwok, K. O., Cao, L., Luong, S., & Tam, W. (2024). The importance of transparency: Declaring the use of generative artificial intelligence (AI) in academic writing. *Journal of Nursing Scholarship*, *56*(2), 314–318.

Veale, M., & Binns, R. (2017). Fairer machine learning in the real world: Mitigating discrimination without collecting sensitive data. *Big Data & Society*, *4*(2), 2053951717743530.

Voigt, P., & Von dem Bussche, A. (2017). The EU general data protection regulation (GDPR). In *A practical guide* (1st ed., Vol. 10). Springer International Publishing.

Wang, Z., Shi, L., & Zhou, C. (2025). Federated privacy preservation algorithm combining conditional generative adversarial network and knowledge distillation. *Egyptian Informatics Journal*, *32*, 100830.

Wilson, K., & Caliskan, A. (2025, April 25). Gender, race, and intersectional bias in AI resume screening via language model retrieval. *Brookings*. https://www.brookings.edu/articles/gender-race-and-intersectional-bias-in-ai-resume-screening-via-language-model-retrieval/

Wu, X., Duan, R., & Ni, J. (2024). Unveiling security, privacy, and ethical concerns of ChatGPT. *Journal of Information and Intelligence*, *2*(2), 102–115.

Zakir, M. H., Bashir, S., Nisar, K., Ibrahim, S., Khan, N., & Khan, S. H. (2024). Navigating the legal labyrinth: Establishing copyright frameworks for AI-generated content. *Remittances Review*, *9*(1), 2515–2532.

Zarsky, T. Z. (2016). Incompatible: The GDPR in the age of big data. *Seton Hall Law Review*, *47*, 995.

Žliobaitė, I. (2017). Measuring discrimination in algorithmic decision making. *Data Mining and Knowledge Discovery*, *31*(4), 1060–1089.

ABOUT THE AUTHORS

Ekta Sinha, SFHAE, is a Lecturer at the School for Business, Regent's University London, UK. She holds a PhD from the prestigious Jamnalal Bajaj Institute of Management Studies, Mumbai, India. Her research interests revolve around three pillars: human-centred innovation, human-centred technology, and sustainability. She has conducted cross-functional research to gain a comprehensive understanding of the interrelated aspects of innovation, sustainability, technology, and human behaviour. She has published papers and teaching cases on human resource management, information systems, sustainable strategy, entrepreneurship, and intrapreneurship in several international refereed outlets such as *Business Strategy and Development*, *Online Information Review*, *Journal of Management Development*, Ivey Publishing, *International Journal of Management Education and Sustainable Development*, among others. She has presented her work in reputed national and international conferences such as the Academy of Management, British Academy of Management, Indian Academy of Management, International Conference on Theory and Practice of Electronic Governance, among others. Her experiences also include coaching professionals on careers, sustainability, and entrepreneurship.

Shalini Chandra is a Full Professor at S P Jain School of Global Management, Singapore. Prior to joining S P Jain, she worked as a Research Fellow at Nanyang Technological University, Singapore, and holds a PhD from the same university. Her research has been published in several international refereed journals such as *MIS Quarterly*, *Journal of Management Information Systems*, *Journal of the Association for Information Systems*, *Information Systems Journal*, *European Journal of Information Systems*, *Communications of the AIS*, among others. She has also presented her work at several top-tier conferences in information systems, such as the International Conference on Information Systems, the Academy of Management, the Pacific Asia Conference on Information Systems, and the Americas Conference on Information Systems, and top-tier communication conferences such as the International

Communication Association. Her research interests include technology-enabled innovation and new collaborative technologies, the adoption and acceptance of new technologies, the dark side of technology, and social media. She currently serves as the Associate Editor at the *European Journal of Information Systems*.

Charles David Waghmare has over 15 years of experience in the information technology, engineering, and energy sectors; he has built a robust career in information management. Since 2019, he has been an Information Management Consultant in the Microsoft 365 space for a global energy leader. Previously, he spent eight years at Capgemini in various roles, including Viva Engage Community Manager and Manager of the Drupal-based Enterprise Knowledge Management system. At Capgemini, he also developed a SharePoint Online knowledge management platform for the Digital Customer Experience organisation and adopted Microsoft Azure Chatbots to enhance customer communication. His career includes a five-year tenure at ATOS (formerly SIEMENS Information Systems Limited), where he managed SAP-based communities using Technoweb 2.0 and on-premises SharePoint. He also served as the global rollout manager for a structured document-management system. An accomplished author, he has written several books on Microsoft 365 technologies, including Viva Engage, SharePoint Online, Azure Chatbots, and ChatGPT. In his spare time, he enjoys reading motivational books, with *The Monk Who Sold His Ferrari* being his favourite.

Printed and bound by CPI Group (UK) Ltd, Croydon, CR0 4YY
24/09/2026
14968847-0001